State-Owned Enterprises and Corruption

WHAT ARE THE RISKS AND WHAT CAN BE DONE?

OECD
BETTER POLICIES FOR BETTER LIVES

Please cite this publication as:
OECD (2018), *State-Owned Enterprises and Corruption: What Are the Risks and What Can Be Done?*, OECD Publishing, Paris.
https://doi.org/10.1787/9789264303058-en

ISBN 978-92-64-30304-1 (print)
ISBN 978-92-64-30305-8 (PDF)

Photo credits: Cover © marigold_88/iStock/Thinkstock

Corrigenda to OECD publications may be found on line at: *www.oecd.org/about/publishing/corrigenda.htm*.

Preface

Today more than a fifth of the world's largest companies are state owned. State-owned enterprises (SOEs) play an important role in the global economy, particularly in key sectors such as public utilities, as well as natural resources, extractives and finance. They take different corporate forms – often combining commercial and non-commercial objectives – with increasingly international operations. Good governance of SOEs is critical for ensuring a level playing field in the marketplace, safeguarding the integrity of domestic economies, and supporting quality public service delivery.

Good corporate governance of SOEs, in accordance with the *OECD Guidelines on Corporate Governance of State-Owned Enterprises*, is also essential to help reduce the risk of corruption. In recent years, we have seen how corruption involving SOEs can cause serious economic and political damage and lead to a breakdown of public trust extending well beyond the SOEs themselves. This is why we need a concerted effort to stamp out corrupt and otherwise irregular practices in SOEs, as well as in government institutions exercising state-ownership rights.

This report, *State-Owned Enterprises and Corruption*, brings a comprehensive set of facts and figures to the discussion about the concrete risks facing SOEs and how they, and their state owners, go about addressing them. It will help shape an international debate that has, until now, been largely anecdotal. Based on the inputs of almost 350 members of executive management and boards of SOEs in OECD and partner countries, the report tracks the experiences of companies facing corruption and the challenges encountered by their management in making SOEs more efficient and transparent. It further charts the legal and institutional frameworks as well as concrete practices of OECD and non-OECD economies in ensuring high standards of governance and accountability in the SOEs they oversee.

The challenge is daunting. Two in five corporate insiders report to have personally witnessed corruption or irregularities in their companies in recent years. The number is even higher in SOEs operating in "high-impact sectors" such as extractives and public utilities where the value of concessions and public procurement contracts is typically large, despite the fact that many of these companies had implemented internal controls. This report examines why these internal controls did not work, looking for answers both within the SOEs and in the "grey zone" between the companies and their state owners.

A core component of the solution is to improve the way in which the state exercises its ownership rights, appoints the governing bodies of SOEs and communicates with the companies. The OECD is leading a convergence in the field of SOE governance and anti-corruption, identifying good practices in this report that will lay the foundation for new guidance for the state that goes beyond existing international standards. This process is taking place in co-operation with the G20, international organisations and civil society.

I encourage all governments to consider what the report's findings mean for the way in which they exercise ownership in SOEs, and participate in this important process of developing guidelines that contribute to stamping out corruption in this vital part of the corporate economy.

Angel Gurría

OECD Secretary-General

Foreword

Corruption is the antithesis of good governance, and it is a direct threat to the purpose of state ownership. This report brings a comprehensive set of facts and figures to the discussion about the corruption risks facing state-owned enterprises (SOEs) and how they, and state ownership, go about addressing them. It is a first step towards developing guidance on anti-corruption and integrity in SOEs for the state as owners. This initiative is rooted in the OECD Guidelines on Corporate Governance of State-Owned Enterprises, the world's sole internationally agreed standard for how governments should exercise its ownership rights over SOEs.

This stock-taking report integrates responses from almost 350 SOEs in 34 countries and state responses from 28 countries, together covering Argentina, Brazil, Canada, Chile, Colombia, Costa Rica, Czech Republic, Denmark, Finland, France, Hungary, Greece, Iceland, Israel, Italy, Japan, Kazakhstan, Korea, Latvia, Lithuania, Mexico, the Netherlands, New Zealand, Norway, Pakistan, Paraguay, Peru, Philippines, Poland, Russia, Slovak Republic, Slovenia, Spain, Sweden, Switzerland, Turkey and the United Kingdom.

The report was prepared by Alison McMeekin with oversight from Hans Christiansen, both of the Corporate Affairs Division in the OECD Directorate for Enterprise and Financial Affairs. It was developed in an ongoing discussion with the OECD Working Party on State Ownership and Privatisation Practices (Working Party), as part of the Working Party's ongoing initiative on supporting state-owned enterprise (SOE) reform in OECD and partner countries. A preliminary version was subject to a multi-stakeholder consultation during a Special Roundtable of the Working Party in October 2017, gathering additional input from participants including the OECD's consultation partners, Supreme Audit Institutions (SAIs), civil society and other international organisations. The report benefitted from the expertise and inputs of colleagues in the Public Sector Integrity Division of the OECD Public Governance Directorate and the Anti-Corruption Division of the OECD Directorate for Enterprise and Financial Affairs.

Table of contents

Tables

Figures

Boxes

Executive Summary

State-owned enterprises (SOEs) are a main conduit for states to exercise their role as economic actors. The benefits of SOE ownership are economic, political and social. So too are the costs of any mismanagement or abuse. Today, SOEs account for 22% of the world's largest companies and are often concentrated in sectors with strategic importance for the state and society, including for development. More and more, SOEs operate like similar private firms, increasingly active internationally and accounting for a greater market share.

The more pronounced presence of SOEs in the global marketplace has been marked by certain high-profile scandals and occasional evidence of a susceptibility of SOEs to corruption. This raises questions about what might make SOEs susceptible to corruption and how policy makers can act to maximise SOE productivity by raising their integrity.

The report answers these questions in two ways:

- Through an analysis of the perceptions and recent experiences of 347 high-level SOE officials and board members.
- Through a review of legal frameworks and approaches at the state level as reported by representatives of 28 national state-ownership agencies or ministries.

Together, the two surveys span 37 OECD and non-OECD countries. They focus on both the most severe forms of corruption, such as bribery, and on other rule-breaking and irregular practices that are harmful in their own right and that may be representative of both corporate and public governance gaps.

The risk of corrupt practices

In almost half of the participating SOEs (and 42% of all respondents), at least one respondent reported that corrupt and related irregular practices have materialised in their company in the last three years. In the last year alone, 47% of all company representatives reported losing an average of 3% of annual corporate profits to corruption and other irregular practices. Companies that received claims through claims and advice channels in the last 12 months have estimated that 40% were linked to corruption or related irregularities.

These perception data provide a strong indication that the threat of corruption and irregular practices in and around SOEs is real. Digging deeper, this report compares companies' perceived experiences with corruption in the last three years with their risks and challenges of the present. From the survey, the following key findings suggest themselves:

- The instances of corruption that were reported most often involved non-management employees and mid-level management. Executive management, charged with their oversight, reported to have witnessed less corruption and fewer irregularities in their company compared to other categories of respondents –

despite being, in some cases, from the same company and despite reporting similar corruption risks and obstacles as their fellow respondents.

- Respondents in oil and gas, mining, postal, energy and transportation and logistics sectors report to have witnessed corrupt and other irregular practices more often than average. These sectors are mostly highly regulated, may have natural market monopolies and are engaged in high-value public procurement projects.
- SOEs report that the greatest obstacles to their companies' integrity relate to relations with the government (for instance including a perceived lack of integrity in the public and political sector), and with behaviour (including opportunistic behaviour of individuals that may be internal or external to the company). SOEs report that challenges also arise from ineffective control and accountability (including ineffective internal control or risk management) and, to a lesser degree, the company culture (including a lack of awareness amongst employees of the need for integrity).
- SOEs with public policy objectives – whether well-defined or more implicit – report higher risks of corruption or other irregularities than those that have entirely commercial objectives. For instance, they are more likely to perceive that the risk of undue influence in decision-making will materialise, that they experience pressure to break the rules and that they are challenged by their proximity to government. They also report taking fewer actions to avoid known corruption risks than SOEs with entirely commercial objectives. SOEs with public policy objectives disclose financial assistance received from the state, including guarantees and commitments, less often than SOEs with entirely commercial objectives.
- SOEs with commercial objectives are more likely to see the allocation of operational budget to integrity as more of an investment or asset than SOEs with public policy objectives. Overall, SOEs see financing integrity as more of a cost or expense than private companies.
- In face of known corruption risks, SOEs generally appear less risk averse or less about to take action than private companies. This could reflect the fact that SOEs are legally obliged to conduct certain activities and consequently have less freedom than private firms to walk away from dubious propositions

Corporate insiders of private firms may face many of the same incentives and opportunities to engage in corrupt practices as those in SOEs. However, this report provides perception-based evidence that some of the risks are increased for SOEs. Opportunistic behaviour leading to corruption may be derived from a "too public to fail" mentality in which SOEs are protected by their state ownership, their market dominant position or their involvement in the delivery of public services, and are insulated from the same threat of bankruptcy and hostile take-over that private companies face. Opportunistic behaviour may also arise out of SOEs' operations in sectors with high value and frequent transactions or within complex regulatory frameworks that, unless well-designed, can provide a smokescreen for non-compliant behaviour.

Internal or external pressures, such as undue influence by the state in SOE operations, may further put employees and managers under pressure to break rules and/or provide opportunities to exploit their position. On the one hand, SOEs with public policy objectives may be more able to justify illicit activity to compensate for financial losses or reduced profit margins that can be associated with delivering on policy objectives. On the other hand, SOEs (and other firms) with entirely commercial objectives may try to justify corruption because of the pressure to remain competitive or to perform.

Risk avoidance and mitigation by state-owned enterprises

The majority of SOEs have rules and mechanisms in place to mitigate corruption risks. In the last year, SOEs have allocated an estimated 1.5% of their operational budgets to preventing and detecting corruption. Almost half of corporate insiders consider this as an asset or investment, but another 40% believe that the financial and human resources available to invest in integrity are "at least somewhat" inadequate. Just over half of SOE respondents report that their company provides anti-corruption or integrity-related training to all employees, board members and management.

Ninety percent of SOEs treat corruption and integrity risks explicitly in risk assessment, most often categorised as compliance risks. Those that conduct risk assessments on an annual basis, as is most common, report fewer risks and consider their internal control and risk management systems to be more effective than those who conduct such assessments less regularly or not at all. Boards and executive management are not always privy to the same internal materials about risks, internal controls or the efficacy of the internal integrity mechanism.

SOEs employ a host of rules and codes to reduce the risk of corruption. Those most common are to do with conflicts of interest, charitable contributions and engagement in public procurement. Some SOEs use a variety of approaches to third-party due diligence, with one third of SOEs having severed a business relationship because of the risk of or exposure to corruption. Most often, SOEs offer multiple channels for complaints, classify them as confidential and report them to the CEO or a board member, or both.

Although the majority of SOEs have some arrangements for risk management and internal control, the evidence in this report demonstrates either a lack of controls, an ineffectiveness of controls, or an override of controls. Investments in integrity may continue to be rendered less effective until the more systemic issue of a lack of a culture of integrity is reversed.

Preventive and remedial action by the state

But what exactly can and should the state do as the owner? The report addresses this question through an analysis of state ownership entities' practices in 28 OECD and non-OECD countries across four continents, insights from Supreme Audit Institutions and comparisons with findings from other international studies. The answer is guided by existing international standards such as the OECD Guidelines on Corporate Governance of State-Owned Enterprises. The Guidelines imply that the state, on a whole-of-government basis, should implement an ownership policy; a designated "ownership entity" within the state should be responsible for defining objectives of individual SOEs and monitoring their performance; the board of directors should be responsible for approving strategy and monitoring management; and the management responsible for the SOE's corporate operations.

SOE respondents reported that relevant national laws, regulations, bylaws or governance codes clearly establish expectations and that the ownership entity clearly communicates expectations regarding integrity and anti-corruption. The majority of ownership entities communicate their expectations through existing laws, provision of supporting documentation (e.g. guidance or memorandums) or further yet, through in-person interactions such as annual general, investor, quarterly or ad-hoc meetings, and increasingly in seminars and workshops.

Anti-corruption and integrity is a specific topic of discussion between some ownership entities and their SOEs, but not all. In a few instances, anti-corruption and integrity is built into the objectives of the company, often couched under requirements for corporate social responsibility. State ownership entities may leave integrity and anti-corruption entirely to the devices of the board under the guise of providing SOEs with functional independence. Conversely, in some countries where SOEs are incorporated in a legal form identical to that of private firms, the authorities take the position that the existent corporate legal framework is, or should be, sufficient in itself to ensure integrity and deter corruption in the SOEs.

Only a handful of ownership entities specifically hire relevant skills, such as audit, compliance or risk management expertise for oversight and monitoring. Co-ordination across relevant public institutions on the subject is largely ad-hoc, with the potential for improving professional relations that strengthen awareness and monitoring of corruption in SOEs as well as measured responses in the case of potential or real corruption. Where it occurs, most ownership entities will act as observer to related investigations, with a few more actively following-up with the SOE upon a case's conclusion.

The report puts forward a number of suggestions for the state as a whole to effectively encourage SOEs to better prevent corruption risks from materialising and detecting them when they do, as well as to enforce the letter of the law accordingly. It must however be emphasised that such efforts will be rendered ineffective if states do not themselves adhere to high standards of integrity.

The report aims to advance the global discussion on corruption in SOEs by pointing the finger not at SOEs alone, but to identifying the obstacles that undermine integrity efforts of both SOEs and their owners. So far, advice on corporate governance has largely focused on performance and implementation of governance arrangements that create the conditions necessary for success. This paves the way for providing further guidance for governments by combining existing corporate governance and anti-corruption instruments, and developing new guidance to shine the light into the previously shaded area between general government and private business in which SOEs are found.

About this report

In 2015 the OECD revised its Guidelines for Corporate Governance of State-Owned Enterprises (the "SOE Guidelines") which supplement and complement the G20/OECD Principles of Corporate Governance (2015a). In 2016, the Working Party on State Ownership and Privatisation Practices ("Working Party") set out to explore whether state-owned enterprises (SOEs) are exposed to unique corruption risks and consequently decided that specific standards of integrity and corporate governance should be developed.

With encouragement from the OECD and other international bodies, the Working Party set out to develop this stock-taking report with the primary objectives of:

- building an evidence base on integrity and anti-corruption risks in SOEs and good practices in countering them, and identifying corruption and integrity risks to SOEs that may either be unique or amplified by state ownership
- taking stock of existing mechanisms used by ownership entities and SOEs to prevent, detect and respond to corruption and irregular practices with the purpose of identifying good practices
- informing future work of the OECD by providing guidance for state ownership entities on the subject.

Scope and definitions

The first two chapters of the report are based on survey responses from large SOEs pursuing significant economic activity, either exclusively or together with public policy objectives. The last chapter is based on survey responses from state-ownership agencies and ministries at the level of national government. This is consistent with the approach of the SOE Guidelines, which, while in principle are applicable to any SOEs, focus mostly on economically significant and commercially-oriented companies. National state ownership entities are encouraged to ask themselves what the findings of this report might imply for the implementation of the SOE Guidelines in their jurisdictions, and to consider what additional steps may be necessary beyond the Guidelines. The SOE Guidelines' definitions for SOE and ownership are set out below in Box 0.1.

The report covers challenges and good practices in integrity and anti-corruption at both the state-ownership and company levels – as well as in the interactions across and between levels. The work provides an SOE-specific follow-up to the OECD's *Corporate Governance and Business Integrity: A stocktaking of Corporate Practices* (2015b), which focused primarily on large, privately owned or publicly listed firms, and whose analysis was framed by the G20/OECD Principles for Corporate Governance (2015c).

Box 0.1. Defining an state-owned enterprise: The OECD Guidelines on Corporate Governance of State-Owned Enterprises

SOE: The SOE Guidelines recognise that any corporate entity recognised by national law as an enterprise, and in which the state exercises ownership, should be considered as an SOE. This includes joint stock companies, limited liability companies and partnerships limited by shares. Moreover statutory corporations, with their legal personality established through specific legislation, should be considered as SOEs if their purpose and activities, or parts of their activities, are of a largely economic nature.

Ownership and control: The SOE Guidelines apply to enterprises that are under the control of the state, either by the state being the ultimate beneficiary owner of the majority of voting shares or otherwise exercising an equivalent degree of control. Examples of an equivalent degree of control would include, for instance, cases where legal stipulations or corporate articles of association ensure continued state control over an enterprise or its board of directors in which it holds a minority stake. Conversely, state influence over corporate decisions exercised via bona fide regulation would normally not be considered as control. Entities in which the government holds equity stakes of less than ten percent that do not confer control and do not necessarily imply a long-term interest in the target company, held indirectly via independent asset managers such as pension funds, would also not be considered as SOEs. For the purpose of these Guidelines, entities which are owned or controlled by a government for a limited duration arising out of bankruptcy, liquidation, conservatorship or receivership, would normally not be considered as SOEs. Different modes of exercising state control will also give rise to different governance issues. Throughout the Guidelines, the term "ownership" is understood to imply control.

Source: OECD (2015a), OECD Guidelines on Corporate Governance of State-Owned Enterprises, 2015 Edition, OECD Publishing, Paris, www.oecd.org/corporate/guidelines-corporate-governance-soes.htm.

The report is steered by use and consistent application of key terms, which makes an important distinction between corruption and other irregular practices, as shown in Figure 0.1. The focus of this report is on the inner three circles – irregular practices that are, in essence, deviations from integrity that harm SOEs and that open avenues for corruption, and specific forms of corruption, including bribery.

Figure 0.1. Defining irregular practices and corruption for the purposes of the report

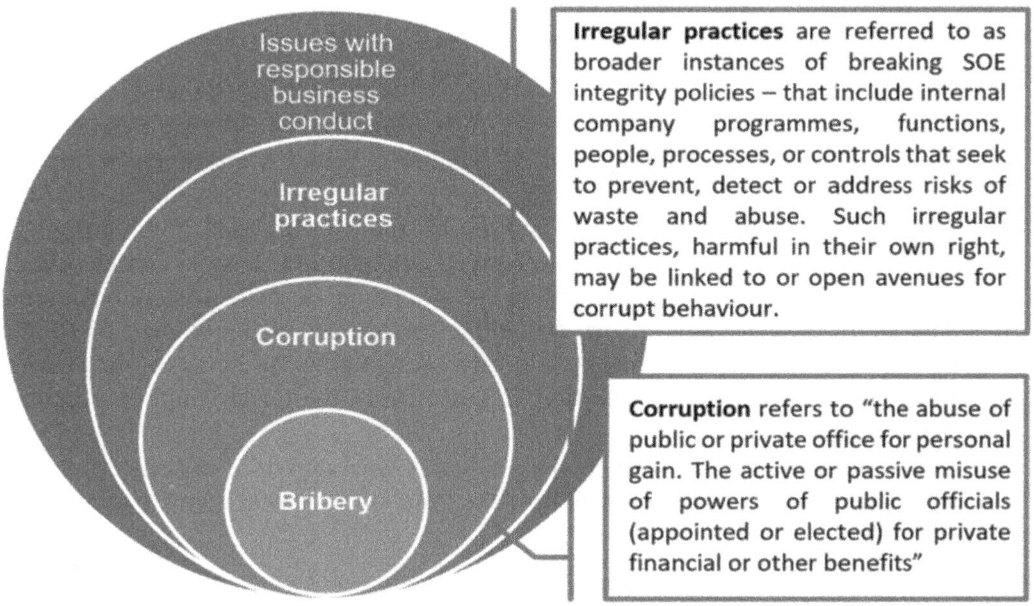

Source: Regarding irregular practices: Adapted from insights in *Corporate Governance and Business Integrity: a Stocktaking of Corporate Practices* (OECD, 2015b). Regarding corruption: while there are various definitions of the concept, this particular one is an adaptation from the OECD's (2008) "Corruption: *A Glossary of International Standards in Criminal Law*", OECD Publishing. Other commonly cited definitions are issued by the World Bank, defined as "the abuse of public office for private gain" and by Transparency International as the "misuse of entrusted power for private gain".

This report makes no reference to the jurisdiction in which irregular practices, corruption or bribery occurs. The report refers to OECD findings about foreign bribery where they are instructive for the broader narrative and understanding of corruption and other irregular practices in SOEs. Suggestions to improve integrity found in this report should be of concern to large, economically-significant SOEs and to their state owners – regardless of the jurisdictions in which they operate.

Responsible business conduct is a key pillar of the SOE Guidelines. The topic is well covered by other OECD instruments, notably the 2011 OECD Guidelines for Multinational Enterprises, and by initiatives on responsible business conduct, and has thus been left outside the scope of this report.

This review benefits from the wealth of existing OECD work on the topic of anti-corruption and integrity, notably that which falls under the auspices of the Working Party of Senior Public Integrity Officials and the Working Party of the Leading Practitioners on Public Procurement of the OECD's Public Governance Committee, and the Working Group on Bribery in International Business Transactions responsible for the monitoring and implementation of the OECD Convention on Combating Bribery of Foreign Public Officials in International Business Transactions (Anti-Bribery Convention).

Methodological approach

The report is based on two surveys – of SOEs and of state ownership entities – together totalling participation of 37 different countries. Respondent characteristics are presented in Annex A.

- The confidential, online SOE survey was filled in by 347 anonymous SOE representatives from 213 SOEs in 34 countries. With 58 questions in the SOE survey (Annex B), the database totals over 20,000 data points, making it one of the largest SOE-specific perceptions survey in the international community. The respondents are board members, executive managers and those in charge of legal, audit, risk or compliance, representing the more than 16 sectors listed in Annex A. The SOE data in this report are either presented as individual respondent perceptions about their companies, or are presented at the company level where possible, depending on the question. In some cases, there were multiple responses per company.
- The ownership survey was filled in by 28 state ownership or co-ordination agencies exercising the ownership on behalf of the state – 25 of which are OECD member countries.

Given the variance in sample sizes of respondents and companies (see Annex A), the report does not claim to be representative of the global situation of anti-corruption and integrity in SOEs. The database does not include responses from 10 companies in each OECD member country that were originally sought. There may be respondent bias insofar as company representatives that opted to participate in the survey, which was voluntary, may have been more aware of the need for integrity and more attuned to the related challenges – whether resulting from a scandal or from demonstrable success in promoting integrity in the company, industry or country. The report does, however, provide evidence of common challenges and solutions across SOEs, and state-owned entities that should not be ignored, but instead considered vis-à-vis the individual risk profile of a company and the ownership structure of a country.

Structure of report

The report is structured in three parts. The first two chapters are primarily informed by the confidential survey of SOE respondents, while Chapter 3 is primarily informed by the state responses to the ownership questionnaire:

1. Chapter 1: exploration of experiences with and perceptions about corruption and other irregular practices in SOEs, assessment of corruption-related risks and elaboration of specific high-risk areas;
2. Chapter 2: elaboration of key elements of anti-corruption and integrity mechanisms or programmes, and existing obstacles to their effective implementation;
3. Chapter 3: discussion on what the state as owner can and should do to promote integrity, given existing OECD recommendations to act as an active and informed owner, but avoiding hands-on intervention in individual SOEs.

Chapter 1. The risk of corruption in and around state-owned enterprises: What do we know?

Based on a survey of 347 SOE respondents from 213 companies in 34 countries, this chapter outlines where corruption and other irregular practices in SOEs have occurred in recent years. It explores how SOE and respondent characteristics, such as the company's sector or the respondent's position, influences the perception of corruption-related risks. Data is deconstructed to understand more about the specific high-risk areas of public procurement, conflict of interest, influence in decision-making and bribery. Concluded cases of corruption and other irregular practices illustrate how such corruption risks can materialise.

Overview: The risk of corruption in and around state-owned enterprises

This section summarises and highlights the main findings from the remainder of the chapter. The chapter deconstructs corporate insiders' perceptions about the risks of corruption and other irregular practices in their SOE. Respondents rated the likelihood and impact of corruption-related risks materialising in their company, as well as whether they believed they had already materialised in the last three years. Respondents' risk assessments, which can be influenced by their past experiences, illustrate where SOE leaders are concerned. The chapter drills down on key risk areas, including public procurement and contracting, conflict of interest, undue influence, favouritism and bribery. The chapter's main findings are as follows:

Forty-two percent of 347 SOE respondents report that corrupt acts or other irregular practices transpired in their company during the last three years, [1] **or at least one respondent in 49% of the 213 companies.** [2]

- SOEs in the oil and gas, mining, postal, energy and transportation and logistics sectors were more likely to have experienced corruption or otherwise irregular practices than companies in other sectors[3] – with between two fifths to one half reporting to have witnessed such practices in the last three years.
- Corruption and other irregular practices reportedly involved all hierarchical levels of the SOE, according to respondents. Those most commonly implicated were non-management employees and mid-level management. Their transgressions occur more in the day to day operations of the company and are thus primarily the responsibility of the Board. Business partners were also implicated according to almost one-third of respondents, highlighting a need for improved third and counter party due diligence and more rigorous application of high standards for subsidiaries, sub-contractors and partners (see Chapter 2 for more on this). One in five respondents saw board members involved in such corruption and other irregular practices, emphasising the responsibility of the state-ownership entity to promote and contribute to sound boards (OECD, 2015a).
- Board members and those in charge of integrity functions (audit, compliance or legal counsel) report seeing corrupt activities and irregular practices more than executive management. As almost half of the participating 213 companies had multiple respondents of different positions fill in the survey, these diverging assessments point to (i) an asymmetry of information as to what happens within the company; or (ii) a difference in executive managements' willingness to report.

The top corruption-related risks facing SOEs are both internal and external to the enterprise. Respondents' assessments of risks differed according to the position of the respondent and their SOEs' sector of operation. Such differing perceptions may have implications for the accuracy of risk assessments and efficacy of associated controls, as well as for reliability and regularity of executive management reporting to the board on corruption risks within the company.

- Respondents consider the top three risks most likely to materialise in their company as: (i) violations of data protection and privacy; (ii) favouritism (nepotism, cronyism and patronage); and (iii) non-declaration of conflict of interest. Those reporting that corrupt or other irregular practices transpired in the company in the last three years also considered violations of data protection and privacy as the top risk. They however deviated by ranking stealing, fraud and receiving bribes, as more likely to occur, which may indicate which risks the respondents saw materialise in their company in the last three years.

- The top 3 risks of corruption and irregular practices considered more impactful for respondent SOEs are: receiving bribes, falsification and/or misrepresentation of company documents, or false accounting and fraud.
- Whether or not respondents had witnessed corruption or other irregular practices did not significantly change how they viewed the likelihood or impact of future risks occurring. SOEs with public policy objectives were less likely to report that corruption risks transpired in their company, compared to SOEs with entirely commercial objective, however, they see the risk of future occurrence to be slightly higher.

The data presented in this chapter, when compared with other international studies on both SOEs and the private sector, suggest that SOEs may be susceptible to corrupt or irregular practices that emanate from both within an SOE as well as by external forces. Particular attention could be placed on non-management employees and mid-level management, as well as executive management charged with their oversight, and highly lucrative industries dealing with natural resources and infrastructure.

Corruption and other irregular practices in state-owned enterprises: What we know

SOEs have been in the spotlight in recent years in view of their increasing international presence and market share. They have also been under scrutiny for corruption and other irregular practices in and around SOEs, with an increasing amount of literature on the potential for undue influence, bribery and other infractions to interfere with the daily operations of an SOE. The OECD's 2014 Foreign Bribery Report found that SOE officials were more often promised or given foreign bribes, and of a higher financial value, than any other public official in all concluded cases of foreign bribery of public officials between 1999 and 2014 (OECD, 2014). A study conducted by the International Monetary Fund (IMF) found that 30% of its mission chief respondents viewed corruption to be widespread in the real sector - 71% percent of whom attributed it to malpractices in the state-owned enterprise sector (IMF, 2017).

Of the 347 respondents in this survey, 42% report that corruption risks materialised into activity or action in their company in the last three years. Aggregated at the company level, at least one respondent in 49% of the 213 surveyed companies reported their materialisation. Irregular practices are also considered in this report, taken to mean activities or behaviours that range from explicit corruption to other offenses, such as stealing that are representative of a lack of ethical behaviour which may be representative of systemic issues that inhibit a culture of integrity.

The proportion of those witnessing corruption or other irregular practices in SOEs, as reported here, appears higher than other studies that also attempt to measure the incidence of corruption and misconduct in both SOEs and other non-state firms, though the results cannot be directly compared. The 2015 Global Business Ethics Survey found that 33% of surveyed private, state and non-profit entities observed misconduct, of which 16% was bribery and corruption related. Twenty-eight percent was talent-related misconduct, 31% was fraud, lying and stealing, 31% was regulatory-type violations, and 21% contracts-related misconduct (Ethics Compliance Initiative [ECI], 2015).[4]

So why is it that SOEs seem more susceptible to corruption or other irregular practices than privately incorporated companies? The remainder of this section looks at perceptions about who is involved in corruption and other irregular practices within SOEs,and where it more commonly happens.

Who perceived corruption, and who did they say was involved?

As mentioned, corrupt and other irregular practices materialised in almost half of the respondents' SOEs in the last three years, reported most often by board members, and heads of the corporate audit, compliance or legal functions (Table 1.1). Almost half of "other" respondents, predominantly corporate secretaries, also reported occurrence of corrupt or irregular practices in the last three years.

Almost half of companies in the sample had multiple respondents. Thus, different experiences between positions or colleagues, with regards to witnessing corruption or irregular practices, suggests either: (i) asymmetry of information within the company, which may be appropriate depending on the respondent's position; (ii) over-reporting; or (iii) under-reporting.

Table 1.1. Those who reported witnessing corruption and other irregular practices, by position of respondent

Responses to: "in your assessment, did any of the [listed] risks materialise into activities/actions in the last three years in (or involving) your company?"

Respondent Position	% of group that responded affirmatively
Board members	43%
Executive management	36%
Heads of corporate audit, compliance or legal functions	45%
Other	46%
Average	42%

Note: Board members includes Chairs and other board members; Executive management includes Chief Executive Officers/Presidents/Managing Directors, Chief Financial Officer or similar or other "C-suite" executives; the group of heads of the corporate audit, compliance or legal functions also included Chief Risk and Chief Sustainability Officers. "Other" refers predominantly to Corporate Secretaries.
Source: OECD 2017 Survey of anti-corruption and integrity in SOEs.

A comparatively limited 36% of executive management respondents reported seeing corruption risks and other irregular practices materialise in their company in the last three years. The apparent difference between executive management responses and the other categories may occur for the following reasons:

- Where corruption has occurred, employees were most often involved (69%). Executive management may lack awareness of non-management employees' behaviour, leaving this to middle management who are also often involved. However, the majority of companies' reporting structures have the unit responsible for integrity most often reporting to the CEO or President, suggesting that the latter has venues through which it could be well informed (discussed in Chapter 2).
- Forty-two percent and 25% of respondents saw mid-level management and senior management, respectively, involved in corrupt activities or other irregular practices. It is possible that executive management representatives reported seeing less corruption (Table 1.1) precisely because of awareness or personal involvement (Table 1.2).
- Executive management may be more likely to under report corruption or corruption risks given their position and responsibility for the company image. Indeed, they

are less likely than other respondents to agree that "loyalty to the company" and "loyalty to customers" can be an obstacle to their company's integrity.

Conversely, board members and those in charge of integrity functions (compliance, audit or legal/counsel), and "other" (mostly corporate secretaries) reported witnessing corruption and other irregular practices more often than executive managers. This may be due to the fact they are often privy to such information through confidential reporting functions.

Table 1.2. Actors reportedly involved in corrupt activities and other irregular practices in state-owned enterprises

Responses to: "Which actors(s) was (were) involved in the corrupt activities/actions / irregular practices that materialised? Please check all that apply."

Which actors(s) was (were) involved?	% of witnesses that have seen the official involved in corruption and integrity-related offenses
Employee	69%
Mid-level management	42%
Business partner	27%
Senior management (executive management)	25%
Board	16%
Public official	14%
Other	10%
Shareholder	8%
Civil society representative	3%

Note: Based on 146 respondents that both reported to have witnessed one of more of the corruption-related activities or integrity offenses put forth, and reported which actors they saw involved.
Source: OECD 2017 Survey of anti-corruption and integrity in SOEs.

Who is involved?

Similar to other international studies on corruption in companies, this study finds that mid-level management and non-management employees are seen as top culprits. Table 1.2 shows that of 146 respondents that reportedly witnessed corruption and other irregular practices in the last three years, 69% reported that non-management employees were involved, followed by 42% who saw mid-level management involved. Around one quarter of respondents said senior management and business partners were involved. It cannot be ignored that 16% of respondents report that corruption risk materialisation involved a board member, 14% a public official and 8% report shareholders. Given the critical roles of boards and the state as a shareholder in promoting corporate governance and preventing corruption, Chapters 2 and 3 deal with improving integrity at these levels.

In one European country, there are three ongoing cases pertaining to corruption allegations with various level courts not yet concluded. All cases reportedly involved improper activities performed by the executive board level and top management of respective enterprises and private contractors. A survey done by the Ethics and Compliance Initiative (ECI) also found that a majority of bribery cases in the private sector involved managers (32% middle managers and 23% top managers).

Who is paying foreign bribes to SOE officials?

The findings of the OECD's Foreign Bribery Report (2014) speaks largely to the role of SOEs in "passive bribery", where SOE officials or board members are offered or given bribes that may or may not have been solicited. SOE respondents to this survey reported that the likelihood of receiving bribes (32% said high or medium risk) was higher than offering bribes (15% said high or medium risk). Respondents see the impact of receiving bribes as higher than offering bribes – though on a smaller margin.

The OECD's 2014 Foreign Bribery Report looked at over 400 concluded cases of foreign bribery. Figure 1.1 displays the level within the company of the person who paid, was aware of or authorised foreign bribery of an SOE official and other public officials from 1999 to 2014. The results suggest that SOE officials are either more susceptible to being offered or given bribes – whether solicited or not – by third parties (agent/consultant) than other public officials implicated in foreign bribery cases, or that they are more likely to solicit bribes from this category than other public officials. On the contrary, SOE officials are less likely to be bribed by or solicit bribes from working level employees than are other public officials.

Figure 1.1. Position of actors who paid, were aware of or authorised foreign bribery of state-owned enterprise officials

Based on concluded foreign bribery cases from 1999 – 2014

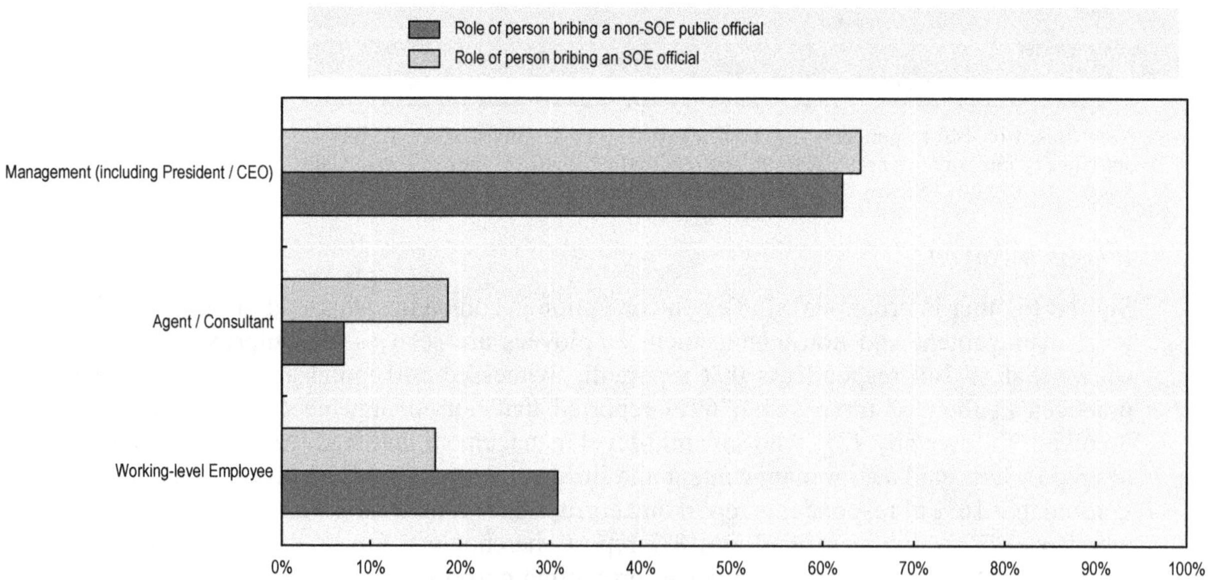

Note: For the purposes of this report, responses of management and President/CEO were merged. The axis represents the percentage of cases involving at least one of the three categories of persons having paid, been aware of or having authorised foreign bribery of public officials.
Source: OECD (2014).

Where is it reported to occur?

Respondents in Latin America reported to witness corrupt and other irregular practices in their companies at a slightly higher rate (47%) than respondents in Europe (43%) and both higher than in Asia (26%).

Respondents in companies with entirely commercial objectives were more likely to report having witnessed corrupt or other irregular practices in the last three years, than respondents in companies with mixed objectives (public policy and commercial). Respondents in both types of company perceive the same likelihood and impact of future risks occurring. Companies with public policy objectives, however, report facing overall greater obstacles to promoting integrity that include: conflicting objectives; pressure to rule-break; opportunistic behaviour of individuals; a perception that the likelihood of getting caught is low; the relations between the company or board and political officials; unclear or ineffective reporting lines between board and others, and; inadequate remuneration or compensation. Respondents in companies with entirely commercial objectives are more likely to face risk of violations of data, regulatory violations, stealing, fraud, and anti-trust or anti-competitive behaviour.

The sector in which a respondent's SOE operates influenced whether the respondent thought that corrupt or other irregular practices transpired in the last three years. The highest proportion of respondents who affirmed this, were found in oil and gas, mining, postal services, energy and transportation and logistics (Figure 1.2).

Figure 1.2. Those who reported witnessing corruption and other irregular practices, by sector of respondent

Sectors of respondents that said "yes" to "in your assessment, did any of the [listed] risks materialise into activities/actions in the last three years in (or involving) your company?"

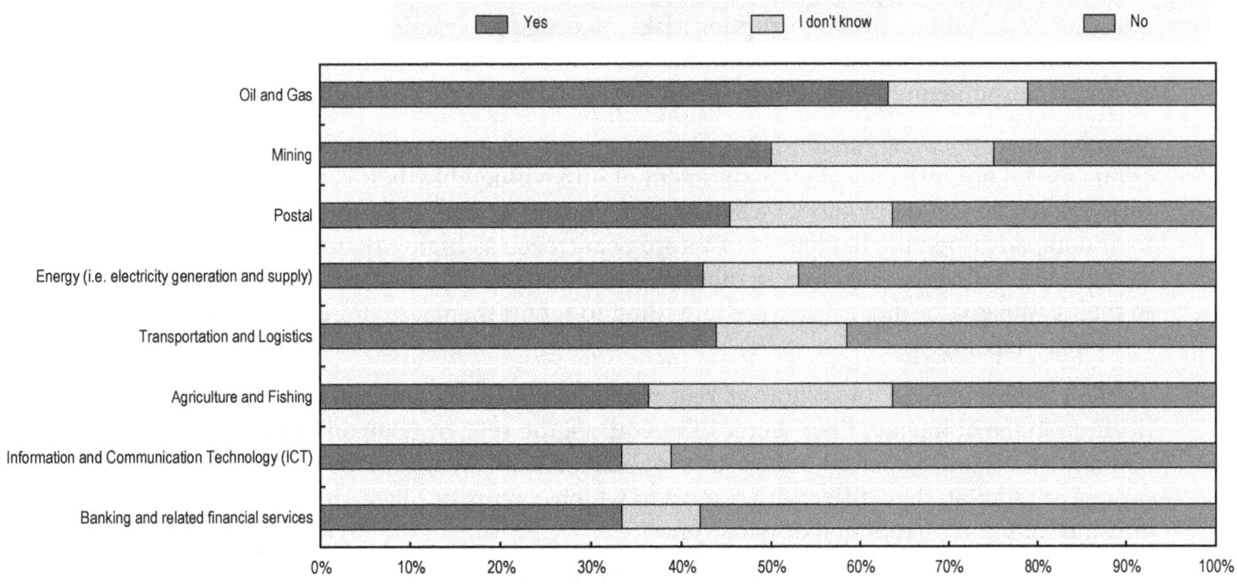

Note: Based on 289 responses falling into the retained 8 categories with more than 10 respondents.
Source: OECD 2017 Survey of anti-corruption and integrity in SOEs.

Some of these sectors are found by other international studies to be at high-risk of bribery, fraud and other economic crimes:

- **Bribery and corruption**: PwC's Global CEO Survey found that CEOs have greatest concern for bribery and corruption in mining, pharmaceuticals, construction, hospitality and energy (PwC, 2016b; 2015b).
- **Economic Crime, including bribery and corruption**: PwC's Global Economic Crime survey (2016a) showed that many of the identified sectors here experienced

increases in economic crime, including bribery and corruption, in the last 2 years - energy, utilities, and mining and transportation and logistics with 6% and 8% increase respectively (PwC, 2016a).

- **Foreign Bribery**: The OECD's Foreign Bribery report showed a higher incidence of foreign bribery in the extractive sector, followed by construction, transportation, and information and communication technologies (OECD, 2014).
- **Fraud, overlapping with corruption**: the Association of Certified Fraud Examiners (ACFE) study of occupational fraud found the highest number of fraud cases that were resulting from, or linked to, corruption, were in mining, transportation and warehousing, oil and gas, manufacturing and technology (ACFE, 2016).

Varying risk perceptions in state-owned enterprises: The likelihood and impact of risks materialising

SOE respondents were asked to assess a range of corruption risks, or risks of integrity offenses, for their likelihood of occurrence and for the impact that the occurrence would have on the company if it were to materialise.[5] The 24 risks put forward for evaluation by respondents is provided in Annex 1.A.

Generally, respondents' rank the likelihood of corruption risks materialising as low, and the impact that their materialisation could have as medium. Despite the anonymity in the survey, a certain self-reporting bias was expected in individuals' responses to this particular question of whether certain corruption risks or irregular practices was likely, for fear of incriminating the company or admitting vulnerabilities to potentially criminal acts. As expected, respondents showed more flexibility in rating impact as higher.

Whether a respondent reported witnessing corrupt or other irregular practices in their company did not influence their assessment of how vulnerable their company is. However, respondents that "did not know" whether such corrupt or irregular practices materialised in their company rated the likelihood of future occurrence as higher than those that were able to provide a definitive response. In other words, those that lack awareness of such activities in their company, or those that were unwilling to report them, are more likely to anticipate risks materialising.

Table 1.3 provides an overview of risk assessments by respondents according to their position in the company, their sector of operation, the type of company objectives and the respondent's (self-declared) status as a public official. While respondents' overall risk ratings are similar, they differ with respect to which corrupt or other irregular practices they consider of higher likelihood of occurrence.

Table 1.4 shows the top 10 corruption risks for their likelihood and impact of occurrence. Four key risks of corruption or irregular practice are explored in further detail below. The risks assigned with the highest likelihood of occurrence are not consistently the same as those assigned the greatest impact on the company. Conversely, some risks considered unlikely to occur were considered to have medium or high impact on the company's ability to achieve key objectives. Only six of ten risks in each category make an appearance as both higher likelihood and higher impact, as shown in Table 1.4.

Table 1.3. Risk assessments by state-owned enterprise respondent characteristics

Respondent category	% of respondents that say risks of corruption or other irregular practices materialised in the last three years	Perceptions of risks of corruption or other irregular practices		
		Likelihood of risks materialising in respondent companies*	**Impact** of risks materialising on respondent companies*	Risks considered more likely to materialise by each category of respondent
All respondents	42%	1.4	2.0	1. Violations of data protection and privacy 2. Favouritism (nepotism, cronyism and patronage) 3. Non-declaration of conflict of interest
Respondent's position in the company				
Board member	43%	1.3	2.1	1. Illegal information brokering 2. Violations of data protection and privacy 3. Favouritism (nepotism, cronyism and patronage)
Executive Management	36%	1.5	2.0	1. Interference in decision-making 2. Procurement/contract violations 3. Violations of data protection and privacy
Heads of the corporate audit, compliance or legal functions	45%	1.4	1.9	1. Violations of data protection and privacy 2. Non-declaration of conflict of interest 3. Procurement/contract violations
Other	46%	1.5	1.9	1. Interference in decision-making 2. Favouritism (nepotism, cronyism and patronage) 3. Violations of data protection and privacy
Respondent's company sector				
Agriculture and Fishing	36%	1.4	1.4	1. Interference in decision-making 2. Favouritism (nepotism, cronyism and patronage) 3. Interference in appointments of board members or CEO
Banking and related financial services	33%	1.4	2.0	1. Non-declaration of conflict of interest 2. Falsification and/or misrepresentation of company documents, or false accounting 3. Receiving bribes 3. Fraud 3. illegal information brokering
Energy (i.e. electricity generation and supply)	42%	1.5	2.2	1. Non-declaration of conflict of interest 2. Procurement/contract violations 3. Receiving kickbacks
Information and Communication Technology (ICT)	33%	1.4	2.0	1. Non-declaration of conflict of interest 2. Violations of data protection and privacy 2. Influence peddling 2. Favouritism (nepotism, cronyism and patronage) 2. Fraud 3. Stealing or theft of goods from the company 3. Receiving kickbacks and/or inappropriate gifts

Respondent category	% of respondents that say risks of corruption or other irregular practices materialised in the last three years	Perceptions of risks of corruption or other irregular practices		
		Likelihood of risks materialising in respondent companies*	**Impact** of risks materialising on respondent companies*	Risks considered more likely to materialise by each category of respondent
Mining	50%	2.0	2.1	1. Favouritism (nepotism, cronyism and patronage) 2. Stealing or theft of goods from the company 2. Fraud
Oil and Gas	63%	1.3	2.1	1. Violations of regulations (health and safety, environmental) 2. Interference in decision-making 2. Fraud 3. Receiving bribes 3. Favouritism
Postal	45%	1.3	1.9	1. Violations of data protection and privacy 1. Stealing or theft of goods from the company 2. Procurement/contract violations 3. Fraud
Transportation and Logistics	42%	1.4	1.9	1. Stealing or theft of goods from the company 2. Procurement/contract violations 3. Violations of data protection and privacy
Respondent's company objectives				
Entirely commercial	49%	1.3	2.1	1. Violations of data protection and privacy 2. Violations of regulations (health and safety, environmental) 3. Stealing or theft of goods from the company
Mixed objectives (commercial with public policy)	36%	1.4	2.1	1. Interference in decision-making 2. Favouritism (nepotism, cronyism and patronage) 3. Non-declaration of conflict of interest
Respondent's status as a public official				
Respondent considered a public official	42%	1.3	2.0	1. Interference in decision-making 2. Favouritism (nepotism, cronyism and patronage) 3. Non-declaration of conflict of interest
Respondent not considered a public official	42%	1.3	2.0	1. Violations of data protection and privacy 2. Procurement/contract violations 3. Non-declaration of conflict of interest

Note: Column 2 - based on responses to: "in your assessment, did any of the [listed] risks materialise into activities/actions in the last three years in (or involving) your company?"; *Column 3 and 4 - based on a constructed index of respondent's ranking of select risks to their company as "low", "medium" or "high", on a scale of 1-3, where 1 = low, 2 = medium and 3 = high. Likelihood is the possibility/probability that a risk event may occur in, or involving, a company. Impact is the affect that the risk event would have on achievement of the company's desired results or objectives. For instance, high impact would have a severe impact on achieving desired results, such that one or more of its critical outcome objectives will not be achieved. Low impact would have little or no impact on achieving outcome objectives; Column 5 - the risks listed in column 5 are ranked in terms of their likelihood of occurrence, noting that in select sectors multiple risks were equally considered as likely to occur and are numbered accordingly.
Source: OECD 2017 Survey of anti-corruption and integrity in SOEs.

Respondents that report to have witnessed corrupt activities or other irregular practices in the present in their company differ with regards to the activities they think might be more likely to materialise (Table 1.5). Notably, those that report having witnessed corrupt or irregular practices in the past rate fraud and receipt of bribes as more likely to transpire than a non-declaration of conflict of interest or favouritism.

Table 1.4. Top reported corruption risks: Perceptions of likelihood and impact of risks materialising

Based on respondents' rankings of select risks (Annex 1.A1) for the likelihood of occurrence in the company and the impact of occurrence

More likely risks	More impactful risks
1. Violations of data protection and privacy	1. Receiving bribes
2. Favouritism (nepotism, cronyism and patronage)	2. Falsification and/or misrepresentation of company documents, or false accounting
3. Non-declaration of conflict of interest	3. Fraud
4. Procurement/contract violations (delivering sub-par goods/services, violating contract terms with suppliers)	4. Offering bribes
5. Interference in decision-making	5. Money laundering
6. Stealing or theft of goods from your company	6. Anti-competitive, anti-trust activities or collusive activities
7. Fraud	7. Illegal information brokering
8. Illegal information brokering	8. Violations of data protection and privacy
9. Receiving bribes	9. Procurement/contract violations (delivering sub-par goods/services, violating contract terms with suppliers)
10. Violations of regulations (health and safety, environmental)	10. Violations of regulations (health and safety, environmental)

Note: Based on responses of 347 individuals, across 213 companies, ranking 24 corruption or other irregular practices for their likelihood of occurrence and the impact if it materialised as low, medium or high. The list of risks put forth for assessment are found in Annex 1.A1.
Source: OECD 2017 Survey of anti-corruption and integrity in SOEs.

Table 1.5. Top reported corruption risks: Based on previous experiences with corruption

Respondents that did not see corruption risks materialise in their company in the last three years	Respondents that did see corruption risks materialise in their company in the last three years
1. Violations of data protection and privacy	1. Violations of data protection and privacy
2. Non-declaration of conflict of interest	2. Stealing or thefts of goods from the company
3. Favouritism (nepotism, cronyism and patronage)	3. Fraud
4. Procurement/contract violations (delivering sub-par goods/services, violating contract terms with suppliers)	4. Receiving bribes
5. Interference in decision-making	5. Favouritism (nepotism, cronyism and patronage)
6. Violations of regulations (health and safety, environmental)	6. Non-declaration of conflict of interest
7. Influence peddling	7. Procurement/contract violations (delivering sub-par goods/services, violating contract terms with suppliers)
8. Receiving kickbacks	8. Illegal information brokering
9. Illegal information brokering	9. Receiving kickbacks
10. Fraud	10, Interference in decision-making

Note: Based on responses of 347 individuals, across 213 companies, ranking 24 corruption or other irregular practices for their likelihood of occurrence if it materialised as low, medium or high. The list of risks put forth for assessment are found in Annex 1.A1.
Source: OECD 2017 Survey of anti-corruption and integrity in SOEs.

SOE respondents were not asked which activities they witnessed due to confidentiality. However, the risks considered more likely to transpire in companies that have, according to the respondents, already experienced corruption or irregularities, may be indicative of what respondents perceived to have witnessed. .

Figure 1.3. Risk heat map of risks of corruption and other irregular practices in state-owned enterprises: Likelihood and impact of occurrence

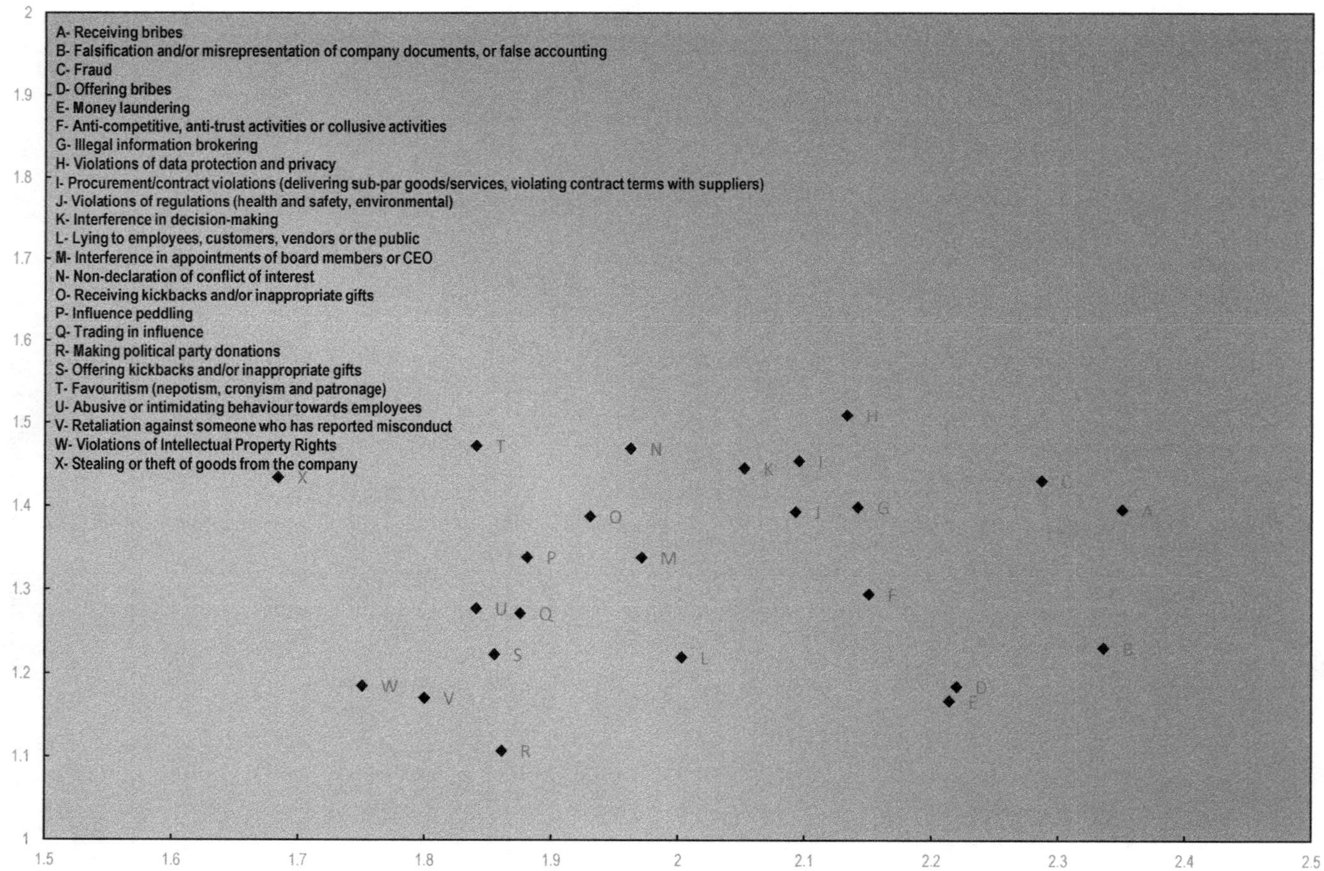

Note: Based on 347 individual assessments of the likelihood of occurrence, and the impact, 24 corruption risks or risks of irregular practices put forth (Annex 1.A1). Both axes represent a perceptions index out of a total of 3, where 1 denotes assignment of "low" impact or likelihood, 2 to "medium" impact or likelihood, and 3 to "high" impact or likelihood. Overall, risk likelihood and risk impact are considered low. The axes of the graph are adjusted to narrow in on key risks.
Source: OECD 2017 Survey of anti-corruption and integrity in SOEs.

To understand the interplay between risk likelihood and impact, a Risk Heat Map of likelihood and impact of risks is presented in Figure 1.3. Where replicated at the company level, plotting a risk tolerance line will help SOEs to determine which risks fall beyond the risk tolerance or risk appetite of the company and thus which are allotted further attention and eventual control. A similar risk mapping exercise could be replicated and tailored to an individual company, using the same corruption risks as put forth in this study, given the new information presented here. Care could be taken to ensure assessments of likelihood are accurate given how survey responses showed variances within the same company. A comparison can be made with the risk tolerance level established by the SOE, or by the state ownership entity. The OECD's *Risk Management by State-Owned Enterprises and their Ownership* shows that the state ownership entity formally set a risk tolerance level for the overall state ownership portfolio in 15% of surveyed countries (OECD, 2016a).

The top 10 risks (Table 1.4), both in terms of likelihood and impact, feature a range of activities that can originate internally within the SOE as well as outside, or with external influence, to the SOE. These high risks can refer to demand (e.g. receiving bribes) and supply (e.g. offering bribes) of corruption.

Box 1.1. Corruption-related risks: A state-owned hospital in Europe

A European SOE provided findings of a recent risk assessment, highlighting the various challenges an SOE can face, including breakdowns of controls that should be in place to protect the SOE from corruption, undue influence and other forms of waste and abuse. The company found a risk of:

- Unequal treatment in decision-making regarding recruitment; recruitment of employees with inadequate qualifications;
- Conflict of interest and biased decision-making in personnel management processes (determination of remuneration, determination of the amount of bonuses); biased decision-making in the appointment of staff;
- Risk of mismatch between purpose and content of missions or training trips; or misplaced and unfounded business trips;
- Ineffective use of entity funds by organising purchases that are not needed for the entity or far beyond the entity facilities;
- Conflict of interest in decision-making; possibility to influence decision-making about the choice of provider;
- Insufficient qualification of employees for the development of quality procurement documentation; contract conditions are not ensured during performance of the contract: implementation of deadlines is not ensured; the order and amount of payments are not observed; goods that are not tendered or not specified in the procurement documentation are purchased; the contract conditions are substantially changed after the completion of the procurement procedure;
- Inappropriate use of the entity's property for personal interests, incomplete accounting of property values, planning of restoring property values, not meeting the interests of the entity on economic grounds;
- Hospital staff faces the public's perception / stereotype in the performance of their duties that it is necessary to present gifts;

Source: OECD 2017 Survey of anti-corruption and integrity in SOEs.

One company provided a frank assessment of the current risks it is facing (Box 1.1), which speaks to challenges within the company as well as those pertaining to interactions with the outside world. This chapter explores below some of the risks highlighted by the company, while Chapter 2 elaborates on how an SOE can insulate itself from, and seek to control, such risks.

Understanding select high-risk areas in state-owned enterprises

As mentioned earlier, at least one respondent in 49% of SOEs reported to have witnessed corrupt and other irregular practices in their company in the last three years. The 347 representatives ranked corruption risks (Annex 1.A1) according to their likelihood and impact of occurrence – pointing to particular risks that are the most pervasive. The findings below on specific corruption risks confirm existing theories on high-risk areas for SOEs, and go further into the details in order to point to circumstances that may make these areas particularly risky.

Where the money is: Procurement and contract violations

The sheer size of public procurement, at 12% of GDP and 29% of public expenditure (OECD, 2017a; 2016b), the volume and regularity of transactions, interactions between public and private spheres, and the potential complexity of the procedures present a risk for public administration, SOEs and private companies, of waste, mismanagement and abuse.

The participation of SOEs in public procurement processes has been of concern to governments and to companies alike – whether as a bidder for public contracts (supplier of goods or services) as well as procurer in the contracting of goods and services (procurer). Between 1999 and 2014, 57% of cases of foreign bribery sought advantages in public procurement. This proportion jumps to 78%, when considering foreign bribery cases involving SOE officials versus those that do not (49%). In other words, SOE officials were more likely to be offered or given a bribe than other public officials and overwhelmingly by actors seeking to obtain procurement contracts.

As shown in previously in Figure 1.3, SOE officials report that the likelihood of procurement or contract violations materialising in the company to be higher than many other risks. Almost 40% of SOE respondents rated the likelihood that procurement or contract violations would occur in their company as high or medium.

Procurement and contract violations, for instance delivering sub-par goods/services, or violating contract terms with suppliers, was rated as amongst the top three risks for respondents:

- in companies operating in energy, postal and transportation and logistics,
- in positions of executive management and heads of compliance, internal audit, legal and similar, but not for board members, and
- that do not consider themselves to be public officials.

The applicability of country guidelines for public procurement to SOEs varies by country. The SOE Guidelines suggest that an SOE should adopt government procurement guidelines when they are fulfilling a governmental purpose (e.g. have public policy objectives) or are a state-owned monopoly. Where SOEs are corporatised and are not subjected to public procurement guidelines, it is not only more important that there is a distinct separation between SOE operations and the state involvement in SOEs, but also that the highest standards are applied in a company's internal procurement and purchasing policy.

The SOE Guidelines recommend that "when SOEs engage in public procurement, whether as bidder or procurer, the procedures involved should be competitive, non-discriminatory and safeguarded by appropriate standards of transparency" (OECD, 2015).

Companies with specific rules for engaging in public procurement as bidder report to have witnessed less corrupt and other irregular practices transpire in the last three years than those companies that do not have specific rules. About half of SOE respondents report that their company has such specific rules: 90% of which said they are subject to competitive bidding on equal footing with other firms. Those on equal footing reported to have witnessed less corrupt and other irregular practices (40%) than the 10% that admitted they are not subject to competitive bidding (62%).

Two-third of respondents report that their companies have specific rules as procurer. Of those who have specific rules as bidder, 90% are subject to government procurement rules. Respondents whose companies are not subject to public procurement rules as procurer of goods and services reported to have witnessed corrupt and other irregular practices more often (59%) than those who do (44%).

Where they are engaging in public procurement as procurer, risks can be mitigated by promoting adherence to public procurement regulations or, where fully corporatised, to adhere to the highest international standards for procurement. When engaging as bidder, having specific rules for bidding may also reduce risk.

Table 1.6. Risks facing state-owned enterprises engaging in public procurement

Act	Specific risks facing SOEs participating in public procurement
Corruption related risks	
Collusion and bid rigging; conflict of interest and undue influence in decision making	• Anti-competitive and "dishonest" behaviour of competitors • Public tender with specific criteria in order to favour a specific supplier • Favouritism • Bidders in the procurement process arrange bidding prices before the tendering call • Bid rigging in local, repetitive small dollar value contracts
Bribery (many respondents referred to "bribery and corruption" together)	• Bribery offered by potential vendors to those participating in the procurement process • Kickbacks • Risks related to money laundering
Other compliance/regulatory, political risk, financial, reputational risks	
Non-compliance	• Lack of awareness or adherence to related regulations
Financial loss and fraud	• Sub-par delivery of services or products, cancellation of contracts, or extension of contract/loss of time • Loss of time and lengthy public procurement procedures arising from disputes
Reputational damage of SOEs and government	• Loss of public trust • Damage to SOE reputation
Sub-par performance	• Contracted sub-standard goods or services / that do not fully meet the needs of the Institution • Supplier complaints

Note: Based on insights from over 50 SOE officials provided written comments on the topic.
Source: OECD 2017 Survey of anti-corruption and integrity in SOEs.

Respondents were asked to elaborate on the particular risks for their company in engaging in public procurement. These are summarised in Table 1.6. While certain political, financial, reputational and other risks were highlighted, the majority focus was on those related to corruption and integrity. SOEs are similarly concerned about bid rigging which undermines the quality of goods and services and increases prices. While bid rigging is not considered corruption, it is illegal in all OECD countries.

In considering how to protect the company from corrupt or collusive activities - either as bidder or procurer - when engaging in public procurement, SOEs could asses the risks that appear throughout the procurement cycle, as reported by OECD's "Preventing Corruption in Public Procurement" (2016b). Further, the "OECD Guidelines for Fighting Bid Rigging in Public Procurement" can provide companies and government with insights into combatting this illegal practice, often linked to broader corruption schemes.

Forty percent of SOEs' integrity functions have the responsibility for third-party due diligence. These companies reportedly witnessed more corruption or irregular practices in their company, than those whose companies' integrity functions do not undertake third-party due diligence. It may be due to the effectiveness of such a function that the respondent is aware of previous infractions. Those with third or counter-party due diligence practices assess that the likelihood and impact of future corruption risks materialising, and their obstacles to integrity, are lower than companies who do not undertake such assessments. Moreover, companies that undertake due diligence assessments report a lower likelihood of procurement violations and anti-trust violations.

The case study (Box 1.2) of a Dutch Railway company illustrates how procurement-related risks can occur in practice. The casualties of the case were not only financial but stemming from a loss of trust by customers in the company. This is also an example where bribery is not a stand-alone infraction but one that is linked to other irregular practices, in this case of sharing confidential information and abuse of position.

Where incentives collide: Conflict of interest

Conflicts of interest (COI) refer, for the purposes of this report, to the influence on decision makers that may detract from the objectives established for the SOE, and/or that serves for personal or political gain. In the public sector, managing conflict of interest aims to ensure that government decisions are not influenced by individual interests. The *OECD Guidelines for Managing Conflict of Interest in the Public Service* state that "while a conflict of interest is not *ipso facto* corruption, there is increasing recognition that conflicts between the private interests and public duties of public officials, if inadequately managed, can result in corruption" (OECD, 2004).

SOEs can seek to adequately manage perceived or real conflicts of interest, knowing that a "too-strict approach to controlling the exercise of private interests may conflict with other rights, or be unworkable or counter-productive in practice" (OECD, 2004). A modern approach to managing conflict of interest involves the steps below, implementation of which are tracked in the OECD's "Report on Implementation" (2007):

- identifying risks
- prohibiting unacceptable forms of private interest
- raising awareness of the circumstances in which conflicts can arise
- ensuring effective procedures to resolve conflict-of-interest situations.

The SOE Guidelines treat conflicts of interest explicitly in only one place, saying: "Mechanisms should be implemented to avoid conflicts of interest preventing board members from objectively carrying out their board duties and to limit political interference in board processes" (OECD, 2015a: VII.E.). However, in the corporate world, conflict of interest does not only arise in board decisions.

It is important to recognise that SOEs can never be completely separated from political intervention or politically-motivated ownership practices that may weigh on the decisions made by their boards. In a PwC (2015) survey of over 1400 CEOs of state backed and non-state backed companies, 69% said government and regulators have a high or very high impact on their business strategy. Yet SOEs can and should protect against political interests that are self-serving or service a personal interest group that run counter to the SOE's main goals (OECD, 2015a).

As all SOE decision-makers, including board members and executive management, could become subject to conflict of interest, SOEs and state ownership entities should ensure that adequate mechanisms for addressing conflict of interest, if it does arise, are in place. The SOE Guidelines make clear that professionals concerned should have neither excessive inherent nor perceived conflicts of interest, and should not have limitations on acting in the SOEs' interest. As such, it should render SOEs "free of any material interests or relationships with the enterprise, its management, other major shareholders and the ownership entity that could jeopardise their exercise of objective judgement" (OECD, 2015a).

Board members should disclose any conflict of interest to other board members, and then disclose information on how they are being managed by the board. Conditions for disqualification should also be clear (OECD, 2015a). One element of conflict of interest management is having particular measures in place to prevent political interference on boards – it is discussed at further length in the following section. The findings in this section focus primarily upon the risk of non-declaration of conflict of interest of SOE board members.

Here, the possibility that conflicts go undeclared is used as a proxy to understand the threat of conflict of interest and, eventually, the potential for undue influence. As shown in risk mapping (Figure 1.3), SOE respondents consider the risk of non-declaration of conflict of interest to be higher than other risks considered in this survey, with 40% of respondents reporting it to be of medium or high likelihood that the risk could materialise in their company. In particular, non-declaration of conflict of interest was rated as amongst the top three risks for respondents:

- in companies operating in banking and related financial services and information and communication technology
- in companies with mixed objectives (public policy and commercial)
- that do not consider themselves to be public officials.

Respondents that see non-declaration of conflict of interest as a high or medium risk for their company also see as more likely the following risks: favouritism (nepotism, cronyism and patronage); interference in appointments of board members or CEOs, and; the risk of interference in SOE decision-making. While the above findings cannot prove causality, they do confirm the link between perceived lack of integrity in the public sector with conflict of interest, appointments and influence in execution of board and executive management duties.

Box 1.2. Case study: Breach of Competition Act in the Netherlands

A breach of the Competition Act by the Dutch railway company (Nederlandse Spoorwegen)

The Netherlands Authority for Consumers and Markets (ACM) published its decision regarding the investigation into a possible breach of the Competition Act by the Dutch railway company (NS) in the public procurement concession for the Province of Limburg in 2014. ACM concluded that NS had abused its economically dominant position in the related tender. There have been two violations. First of all, NS made a bid that the ACM qualifies as loss-making and, secondly, there were several non-compliant behavioural actions by NS towards competitors around the tender.

Following a complaint by Veolia (French railway company), the ACM started an investigation in October 2014 into the conduct of NS during the tendering procedure for public transport in Limburg. Following from the ACM investigation, NS came across serious irregularities during an internal compliance investigation. During the tendering process, staff at Qbuzz had received unauthorised confidential information from a (former) employee of Veolia Transport Limburg. In March 2015, the supervisory board instructed its company law firm De Brauw to look into the matter. Certain Qbuzz directors were suspended. The supervisory board also instructed De Brauw to carry out an additional investigation into the possible involvement of the CEO and attempt by the CEO to influence the previous investigation. Based on the findings of this investigation, the supervisory board decided to dispense with the services of the CEO. Further, the chairman of the supervisory board resigned. The financial damage is not quantifiable, but the irregularities had a huge impact not only financially, but it also damaged the trust in NS of passengers, stakeholders and staff.

Impact, Response and future prevention

This case resulted in the departure of the chairman of the board under whose responsibility the irregularities have taken place. In addition, there is a criminal procedure against some former directors and NS.

Commissioned by the supervisory board and the Minister of Finance in one's capacity as shareholder, research and consultancy firm Alvarez & Marsal carried out a thorough analysis of the effectiveness of the existing internal procedures, risk management, compliance and checks within NS and all its subsidiaries. NS has taken additional measures based on the Alvarez & Marsal report to refine internal procedures and checks and it has drawn up an action plan preventing bribery and corruption in the future.

The board of directors of NS has been expanded with a portfolio holder Governance, Risk and Compliance. Internal procedures and codes of conduct for procurement (and compliance with them) have been tightened.

Source: Materials provided by the Ministry of Finance of the Netherlands.

Conflict of interest rules

Respondents in companies with conflict of interest (COI) rules are slightly more likely to report having seen corruption or other irregular practices transpire in the last three years compared to companies without specific conflict of interest rules (42% versus 40%, respectively). However, respondents in companies with COI rules think it is less likely that conflicts would go undeclared in the present or future. Companies who report that non-declaration of COI is more likely to occur face obstacles to integrity that are more to do with company reputation, and proximity to government. For instance, these respondents report the following obstacles to integrity (more than those who do not see non-declaration as an issue):

- a lack of integrity in the public sector
- a lack of clarity in the reporting lines between management and the board
- the relationships between their company or the company's board and political officials to be more of an obstacle to integrity.

It is possible that companies with conflict of interest rules have them in place because of previous instances (in the past three years), and thus judge their future risks as lower. The results suggest that the mere presence of conflict of interest rules alone is not enough to encourage declaration of conflicts.

What next?

The SOE Guidelines state that there may be a case for political oversight of SOEs that are carrying out important public service obligations. Objectivity and professionalism of such political oversight is important, particularly in view of the above findings. For SOEs engaged in economic activities without public policy objectives it is good practice to avoid board representation by the highest levels of political power including from within the government and the legislature, without precluding civil servants and other public officials from serving.

Declaration of conflict of interest of not only the board, but of other decision-makers in an SOE on a cyclical basis would be beneficial to mitigate opportunities for it to go unnoticed.

Where actions are influenced: Interference in decision-making and favouritism in state-owned enterprises

Interference in decision-making is representative of a weakness in controls and in the SOEs' protection from competing interests that detract from its objectives. It is not *ipso facto* corruption, but, like conflict of interest, can represent a situation that may lead to the abuse of entrusted power for private gain. Undue interference may occur in strategic or operational processes, and may be borne out of internal or external forces to the company.

Favouritism, on the other hand, may be a concrete manifestation of conflict of interest or result of influence in decision-making, whereby an individual who has the power to make decisions prioritises personal interest over the interest of the company in actions in the form of nepotism, cronyism or patronage. Favouritism side-steps integrity mechanisms, such as merit-based board or CEO appointments, transparent procurement procedures or active and professional ownership by the state. It may be representative of an underlying conflict of interest, or of other influence in decision-making.

Interference in decision-making was rated as amongst the top three risks for respondents:

- in companies operating in agriculture and fishing and oil and gas
- in positions of executive management and "other" (namely, corporate secretaries)
- that consider themselves to be public officials.

The perceived impact of interference in decision-making was rated as greater than of favouritism, suggesting that interference in decision-making may include, but extend beyond, favouritism.

Respondents that are heads of integrity or "other" (namely, corporate secretaries) assigned higher likelihood to the risk of interference in decision-making and favouritism. This suggests that the decision makers themselves are less aware of the risk of interference in their processes, disagree with colleagues about the likelihood of the risk, or were less willing to report it.

Box 1.3. Case study: Board detection and follow-up in a Colombian state-owned enterprise

This case involves the bribery of a former official of the Colombian state-owned enterprise Ecopetrol S.A, who was in charge of the approval and the assigning of contracts by Ecopetrol S.A. He received bribes from three former executives of PetroTiger Ltd (PetroTiger is a privately held British Virgin Islands company with operations in Colombia and offices in New Jersey) in order to obtain approval to enter into an oil-related services contract.

Detection

In 2010, the Board of Directors of PetroTiger started noticing a series of inconsistencies in the financial and operational results of the company. Subsequently, the Board of Directors conducted an in-depth restructuring process and ordered a forensic external audit. Prior to the audit, the external audit company received training from the Secretariat of Transparency on the scope and aim of the OECD Anti-Bribery Convention, particularly with respect to the role of auditors in the prevention and detection of foreign bribery.

The external audit detected undocumented transactions performed from one of PetroTiger's bank accounts in the United States. The audit findings revealed that, between the period June 2009 and February 2010, three executives paid bribes on behalf of PetroTiger to the Ecopetrol official in order to secure the approval for an oil service contract and to obscure the payments that were made. These payments later involved the official's wife who, while a stylist and owner of a spa in Colombia, received several payments under the guise of business consulting services for the firm that were never performed. In order to secure this oil services contract (worth approximately USD 39.6 million) the ex-executives of PetroTiger paid an amount of around USD 333,500.

Impact, response and future prevention

In Colombia seven prison sentences were given to former employees. Additional actions included fines handed to executives of PetroTiger, debarment of PetroTiger and increased monitoring within Ecopetrol by its compliance division.

Source: OECD (2017c), *The Detection of Foreign Bribery,* OECD Publishing, Paris, www.oecd.org/corruption/the-detection-of-foreign-bribery.htm; and materials provided by the Colombian Ministry of Finance and Public Credit.

Respondents considered to be public officials were slightly more likely to report that the risk of the likelihood of interference in decision-making could occur, but their status had no bearing on the perceived risk of favouritism in the company.

Those who reported a higher risk of interference in decision-making, as well as of favouritism, were more likely to see the "relations between your company or board and political officials" as an obstacle to integrity in their company. Respondents in companies with a higher average proportion of independents on the board, and a lower proportion of political or other state figures:

- rank the risk of interference in decision-making as lower than average
- rank the risk of influence in appointments occurring lower than average
- rank the risk of favouritism occurring as lower than average.

Bribery and personal relations can be used to sway decisions in the best interest of the company. The case (Box 1.3) of a Colombian Oil company shows how bribery, intermingled with favouritism and nepotism, led to sanctioning of one SOE.

Where the bribes are: state-owned enterprise officials receiving, or being offered, bribes

The 2015 revision of the SOE Guidelines contains an explicit reference to preventing corruption: "The boards of SOEs should develop, implement, monitor and communicate internal controls, ethics and compliance programmes or measures, including those which contribute to preventing fraud and corruption. They should be based on country norms, in conformity with international commitments and apply to the SOE and its subsidiaries" (OECD, 2015a: V.C).

One of the most common focuses of the discussion on corruption with regards to SOEs centres on bribery. This was made more prominent following the release of the Foreign Bribery Report (OECD, 2014), which found that SOE officials were bribed in 27% of cases and received 80% of total foreign bribes between 1999 and 2014. The next largest recipient group were heads of state, which were bribed in a total of 5% of cases but received 11% of total bribes. This highlights a vulnerability of SOE officials to foreign bribery over other public officials.

Figure 1.4. The risk of receiving and offering bribes in state-owned enterprises: Likelihood and impact

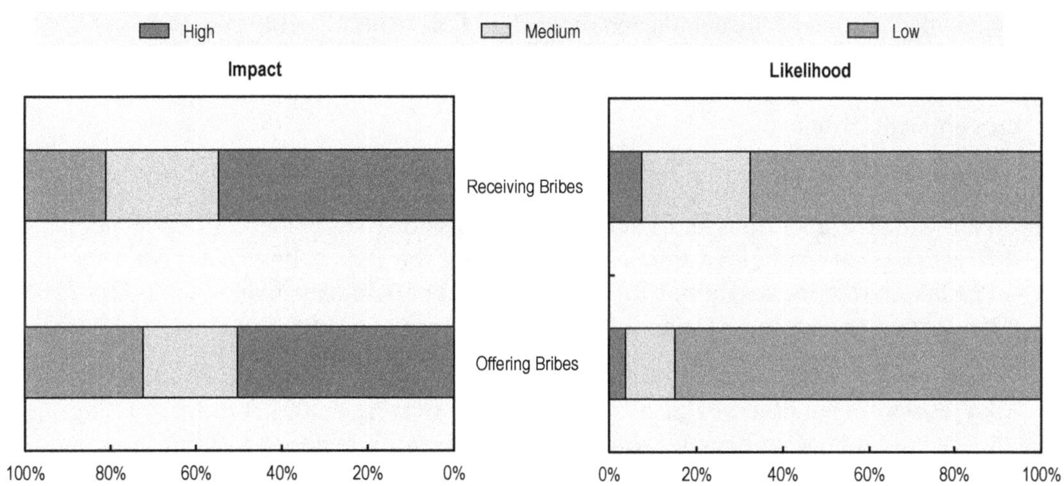

Note: Based on responses of 347 individuals, across 213 companies, ranking the risks of receiving or offering bribes for their likelihood of occurrence and the impact if it materialised as low, medium or high. The list of risks put forth for assessment are found in Annex 1.A1.

Source: OECD 2017 Survey of anti-corruption and integrity in SOEs.

Risk perceptions on receiving bribes

SOEs rate the likelihood of receiving bribes as slightly higher than offering them, but see their negative impact similarly high. Figure 1.4 demonstrates the likelihood and impact of bribery in respondents' SOEs.

Box 1.4. Case study: Bribery

Snamprogetti Netherlands BV ("Snamprogetti") had a 25% participation in the TSKJ Consortium. The remaining participations were held in equal shares of 25% by Halliburton/KBR, Technip and JGC. Since 1994, the TSKJ Consortium has been involved in the construction of natural gas liquefaction facilities at Bonny Island in Nigeria.

Snamprogetti SpA, the holding company of Snamprogetti Netherlands BV, operated as a wholly owned subsidiary of Eni SpA until February 2006, when an agreement was entered into for the sale of Snamprogetti SpA to Saipem SpA (at the relevant time 43% owned by Eni SpA). Snamprogetti SpA was merged into Saipem SpA as of October 1, 2008. In connection with the above-mentioned sale, Eni SpA agreed to indemnify Saipem SpA for losses resulting from the investigations (see section "Detections" below). Eni SpA is 30% owned -- considering direct and indirect participations -- by the Italian Ministry of Economy and Finance.

According to court documents, Snamprogetti authorised the joint venture to hire two agents to pay bribes to a range of Nigerian government officials, including top-level executive branch officials, to assist Snamprogetti and the joint venture in obtaining the Engineering Procurement Contracts (EPC). At crucial junctures preceding the award of contracts, Snamprogetti's co-conspirators met with successive holders of a top-level office in the executive branch of the Nigerian government to ask the office holders to designate a representative with whom the joint venture should negotiate bribes to Nigerian government officials. The joint venture paid approximately USD 132 million to a Gibraltar corporation controlled by one of the agents and more than USD 50 million to the other agent during the course of the bribery scheme. According to court documents, Snamprogetti intended these payments to be used, in part, for bribes to Nigerian government officials.

Detection

In 2004 the US Securities and Exchange Commission (SEC), the US Department of Justice (DoJ) and other authorities, including the Public Prosecutor's Office in Milan, started investigations for alleged improper payments made by the TSKJ Consortium to certain Nigerian public officials between 1995 and 2004.

The company reached a resolution with both the SEC and DoJ. Under the terms of a resolution with the SEC, Eni and Snamprogetti were enjoined from violating the securities laws and agreed to jointly and severally disgorge $125 million of profits. Under the terms of a deferred prosecution agreement (DPA) entered into in July 2010, the DoJ agreed to defer prosecution of Snamprogetti for two years. Snamprogetti, its then parent company, Saipem SpA, and its former parent company, Eni SpA, agreed to ensure that their compliance programmes satisfied certain standards and to cooperate with the DoJ in ongoing investigations. In particular, the companies agreed to conduct a review of their then existing internal controls, policies and procedures in compliance with the DPA. In addition, where necessary and appropriate, the companies further agreed to adopt new or to modify existing internal controls, policies and procedures in order to ensure that it maintained: (a) a system of internal accounting controls designed to ensure that the companies make and keep fair and accurate books, records and accounts; and (b) a rigorous anti-corruption compliance code, standards and procedures designed to detect and deter violations of the Foreign Corrupt Practices Act of 1977 (US federal law) and other applicable anti-corruption laws. The DPA did not require the implementation of any independent compliance monitor (as it occurred, on the contrary, to the other companies participating in the TSKJ Consortium). At the conclusion of the two-year deferral period, all charges against the companies in the United States were dismissed.

Source: Materials provided by the Italian Ministry of Economics and Finance, Department of Treasury.

Receiving bribes was rated as amongst the top three more probable risks to materialise for respondents in banking and related financial services. In addition, receiving kickbacks was a top three for SOEs in the energy sector.

To get a better understanding of who is involved in corruption and bribery, Table 1.7 summarises culprits found in this study as well as in the OECD Foreign Bribery Report and a study by the Ethics and Compliance Initiative. The studies cannot be directly compared due to the different audiences (the latter two focused on more than SOEs), and that this survey did not distinguish specifically whether bribery was observed. However, it becomes clear in all studies that senior management have been involved to a degree. Moreover, Box 1.4 provides a case study that looks at these issues in practice, at improper payments made and the detection and response by the company as a result.

Table 1.7. Which level of the organisation is involved in bribery and corruption? A comparison of various international studies

SOE Survey: % of SOE officials that have seen the following actors involved in corruption-related activities or irregular practices involving their SOE	ECI survey: % of company officials involved in bribery	OECD Foreign Bribery Report: % of officials who paid, were aware of, or authorised foreign bribery
Employee - 69% Mid-level management - 42% Business partner - 27% Senior management - 25% Board - 16% Public official - 14% Other - 10% Shareholder - 8% Civil society representative - 3%	Top manager(s) – 23% Middle manager(s) – 32% First line supervisor(s) – 19% Non-management employee(s) – 16% Public official(s) – 5% Individual(s) outside the organisation – 4%	Management – 41% Non-management – 22% President / CEO – 12% Unknown – 16% Third-party agent – 9%

Note: The categorisations used in the three studies vary and thus their comparison is limited.
Source: OECD 2017 Survey of anti-corruption and integrity in SOEs; OECD (2014), Foreign Bribery Report; Ethics and Compliance Initiative (2016), Measuring Risk and Promoting Workplace Integrity, Global Business Ethics Survey 2016, www.ethics.org/ecihome/research/gbes/gbes-form.

Notes

[1] Out of 343 valid individual responses for this survey question, 146 respondents said yes, 153 said no, and 44 "did not know" whether corruption risks had materialised in their company in the last three years. The weighted average for the sample is also 42%. When dropping all country responses where less than five, or more than the requested ten company responses were provided, this number falls to 39%.

[2] In 106 of 209 companies that provided a response to this question, at least one respondent said yes. When dropping all country responses where less than five, or more than the requested ten company responses were provided, in 45% of companies at least one respondent reported to have witnessed corrupt or other irregular practices in their company in the last three years.

[3] A comparison is made with agriculture and fishing, information and communication technology, and banking and related financial services. While respondents from other sectors participated, responses from sectors with less than ten responses were dropped from the sectoral analysis (aerospace and defence, chemicals, construction and engineering, healthcare, hospitality and leisure, manufacturing, pensions and insurance, real estate, retail and wholesale and other).

[4] A PwC survey of economic crime in 2016 showed that 24% of private companies suffered from bribery and corruption, registering as the third largest form of economic crime behind asset misappropriation (64%) and cybercrime (32%) (PwC, 2016). PwC's 2016 survey of Global Economic Crime includes 6,337 completed surveys across 115 countries in industrial, consumer sectors, technology and other sectors, and financial and professional services.

[5] Likelihood is the possibility/probability that a risk event may occur in, or involve, your company. Impact is the affect that the risk event would have on achievement of your company's desired results or objectives. For instance, high impact would have a severe impact on achieving desired results, such that one or more of its critical outcome objectives will not be achieved. Low impact would have little or no impact on achieving outcome objectives (Georgetown University, 2017)

References

Association of Certified Fraud Examiners (ACFE) (2016), *Report to the Nations on Occupational Fraud and Abuse*, 2016 Global Fraud Survey, www.acfe.com/rttn2016/docs/2016-report-to-the-nations.pdf.

Ethics and Compliance Initiative (ECI) (2016), *Measuring Risk and Promoting Workplace Integrity, Global Business Ethics Survey*, Ethics and Compliance Initiative, www.ethics.org/ecihome/research/gbes/gbes-form.

Georgetown University (2017), Impact, Likelihood and Velocity, https://riskmanagement.georgetown.edu/RiskAssessmentMeasures.

International Monetary Fund (IMF) (2017), *The Role of the Fund in Governance Issues - Review of the Guidance Note - Preliminary Considerations - Background Notes*, Policy Papers, the International Monetary Fund, www.imf.org/en/Publications/Policy-Papers/Issues/2017/08/01/pp080217-background-notes-the-role-of-the-fund-in-governance-issues-review-of-the-guidance-note.

OECD (2017a), *Government at a Glance 2017*, OECD Publishing, Paris, www.oecd.org/gov/govataglance.htm.

OECD (2017b), *The Detection of Foreign Bribery,* OECD Publishing, Paris, www.oecd.org/corruption/the-detection-of-foreign-bribery.htm.

OECD (2016a), *Risk Management by State-Owned Enterprises and their Ownership*, OECD Publishing, Paris, http://dx.doi.org/10.1787/9789264262249-en.

OECD (2016b), Preventing Corruption in Public Procurement, www.oecd.org/gov/ethics/Corruption-in-Public-Procurement-Brochure.pdf.

OECD (2015a), *OECD Guidelines on Corporate Governance of State-Owned Enterprises, 2015 Edition*, OECD Publishing, Paris, www.oecd.org/corporate/guidelines-corporate-governance-soes.htm.

OECD (2015a), *Corporate Governance and Business Integrity: A Stocktaking of Corporate Practices*, OECD Publishing, Paris, www.oecd.org/corruption/corporate-governance-business-integrity-stocktaking-corporate-practices.htm.

OECD (2015b), *G20/OECD Principles of Corporate Governance*, OECD Publishing, Paris, www.oecd.org/corporate/principles-corporate-governance.htm.

OECD (2014), *OECD Foreign Bribery Report: An Analysis of the Crime of Bribery of Foreign Public Officials*, OECD, Paris, www.oecd.org/corruption/oecd-foreign-bribery-report-9789264226616-en.htm.

OECD (2008), *Corruption: A Glossary of International Standards in Criminal Law*, OECD Publishing, Paris, http://dx.doi.org/10.1787/9789264027411-en.

OECD (2007), OECD Guidelines for Managing Conflict of Interest in the Public Service: report on implementation, OECD Publishing, Paris, www.oecd.org/gov/ethics/managingconflictofinterestinthepublicservice.htm.

OECD (2004), "OECD Guidelines for Managing Conflict of Interest in the Public Service", in *Managing Conflict of Interest in the Public Service: OECD Guidelines and Country Experiences*, OECD Publishing, Paris. http://dx.doi.org/10.1787/9789264104938-2-en.

PwC (Price Waterhouse Coopers) (2016a), Adjusting the Lens on Economic Crime: Preparation brings opportunity back into focus, Global Economic Crime Survey 2016, www.pwc.com/gx/en/economic-crime-survey/pdf/GlobalEconomicCrimeSurvey2016.pdf.

PwC (2016b), *Redefining Business Success in a Changing World: CEO Survey*, 19th Annual Global CEO Survey, www.pwc.com/gx/en/ceo-survey/2016/landing-page/pwc-19th-annual-global-ceo-survey.pdf.

PwC (2015a), *State-Owned Enterprises: Catalysts for Public Value Creation*?, www.pwc.com/gx/en/psrc/publications/assets/pwc-state-owned-enterprise-psrc.pdf.

PwC (2015b), *A Marketplace without Boundaries? Responding to disruption*, www.pwc.com/gx/en/ceo-survey/2015/assets/pwc-18th-annual-global-ceo-survey-jan-2015.pdf.

Annex 1.A. List of corruption risks and other irregular practices in the OECD State-Owned Enterprise Survey

Table 1.A1.1: Risks of corruption and other irregular practices: Question options from the state-owned enterprise survey

Response options to the following questions: (i) "in your personal assessment, please rate the below integrity risks for their likelihood of materialising/occurring and the impact they would have on your company?" and (ii) "in your assessment, did any of [these] risks materialise into activities/actions in the last three years in (or involving) your company?"

List of corruption risks and risks of related irregular practices
Anti-competitive, anti-trust activities or collusive activities
Abusive or intimidating behaviour towards employees
(Receiving) bribes
(Offering) bribes
Favouritism (nepotism, cronyism and patronage)
Fraud
Illegal information brokering
Falsification and/or misrepresentation of company documents, or false accounting
Influence peddling
Interference in appointments of board members or CEO
Interference in decision-making
(Receiving) kickbacks and/or inappropriate gifts
(Offering) kickbacks and/or inappropriate gifts
Lying to employees, customers, vendors or the public
Non-declaration of conflict of interest
Money laundering
Procurement/contract violations (delivering sub-par goods/services, violating contract terms with suppliers)
Making political party donations
Retaliation against someone who has reported misconduct
Stealing or theft of goods from your company
Trading in influence
Violations of data protection and privacy
Violations of Intellectual Property Rights
Violations of regulations (health and safety, environmental)
Other, please specify

Note: Likelihood is the possibility/probability that a risk event may occur in, or involve, a respondent's company. Impact is the affect that the risk event would have on achievement of the company's desired results or objectives. For instance, high impact would have a severe impact on achieving desired results, such that one or more of its critical outcome objectives will not be achieved. Low impact would have little or no impact on achieving outcome objectives

Source: OECD 2017 Survey of anti-corruption and integrity in SOEs.

Chapter 2. Promoting integrity and preventing corruption in state-owned enterprises: What works and what does not?

This chapter explores obstacles to effective integrity and anti-corruption in the opinion of 347 SOE respondents in 213 companies across 34 countries. It incorporates the perspectives of SOE representatives and state ownership entities regarding challenges and good practices in implementing mechanisms to prevent and detect corruption. The analysis is framed using key elements of integrity, compliance or anti-corruption mechanisms and programmes, as outlined by the OECD and other international standard-setters – from prevention to detection and response.

Overview: Promoting integrity and preventing corruption in state-owned enterprises

This section summarises and highlights the main findings from this chapter, which outlines the challenges that SOEs are facing in adopting and effectively implementing internationally-recognised elements of compliance and integrity mechanisms and programmes. It deconstructs SOE responses to the 2017 SOE survey on anti-corruption and integrity, assessing which factors may act as obstacles to effectively promoting integrity and preventing corruption in, or involving, respondents' companies.

Four out of five SOEs allocated an average of 1.5% of operational budget to detecting and addressing corruption and breaches of integrity in the last year. The majority of SOEs have internal audit, a degree of public disclosure, assessments of anti-corruption and integrity risks as part of risk management and complaints and advice channels for reporting wrongdoing.

There is more work to be done in adopting and implementing integrity mechanisms that are tailored to the company's risk profile and in increasing their efficacy. Such efforts must be coupled with a culture of integrity to counter pressure and undue influence where corruption is a systemic issue, and opportunistic behaviour by individuals where it is not. The overall findings indicate that certain factors may be pronounced in SOEs.

Participating SOEs' greatest obstacles to integrity relate to behavioural issues and relations with the state. These obstacles are more pronounced for respondents that report having witnessed corrupt or other irregular practices in the last three years. Overcoming these will require strengthening of the ten key elements of effective integrity and anti-compliance programmes that form the basis of this chapter. In particular, it will require:

- Making a clearer argument for investing in preventing, detecting and addressing integrity and anti-corruption, changing the perception that it is a burden or cost. SOEs see budget allocation to preventing, detecting and addressing integrity and anti-corruption as more of a burden than private companies (OECD, 2015a). Despite an average 1.5% allocation of operational budget, some respondents still see inadequate resourcing as at least "somewhat of an obstacle" to company integrity.
- Promoting a culture of integrity within the SOE and at the government level. Respondents ranked "a lack of integrity in the public and political sector" as the primary obstacle for their company. A close second was a "lack of awareness among employees of the need for, or priority placed on, integrity".
- Ensuring professional and transparent SOE interactions with the ownership entity and broader public sector. In addition to reporting the risk of non-declaration of conflict of interest, 27% of SOE respondents voiced concerns about relations between the SOE and political officials.
- Considering opportunistic behaviour and risk-taking in SOEs versus private companies. SOE respondents reported that some of the greatest obstacles to integrity in their company include the opportunistic behaviour of individuals, a pressure to rule-break or to perform and perceptions that (i) the cost of corruption is low, (ii) the return is high, or (iii) they are unlikely to be caught. Comparison with a OECD study on business integrity showed that private sector companies were more likely to have behaved in a risk-averse manner when faced with corruption risks than SOEs of this study (2015a).
- Strengthening internal controls and equipping internal audit. Nearly all companies have some arrangement of integrity mechanisms – controls, detection and reporting

systems – but there are common challenges in their effectiveness. Board members and executive management pointed to a lack of effectiveness in internal controls, audit or risk management as an issue for integrity.

- Explicitly and regularly treating corruption risks. Almost one in ten companies does not explicitly treat anti-corruption risks as part of risk management. SOEs that conduct risk assessments every two to three years were more likely to witness corruption in their company and to report greater obstacles to effective prevention and detection than companies conducting risk assessments annually.
- Ensuring due process for enforcement and, where necessary, sanctioning non-compliance, breaches of integrity and corruption. Demonstrating an SOE's or a state's willingness to enforce high standards of integrity should increase the opportunity cost of engaging in corrupt or other irregular practices. It may also counteract any perception, if and where it exists, that SOEs or corporate insiders are not likely to be caught. It may also facilitate repatriation of funds in cases of cross-border corruption.
- Investing in prevention, detection and enforcement helps to safeguard SOEs from self-serving behaviour that may stem from within an SOE, or from undue influence and exploitation by any third parties. The trifecta of corruption prevention, detection and response should remove blind spots to corruption, and reduce the likelihood of financial losses, risk of non-compliance, loss of trust by clients and citizens and reputational damage. Compliance, integrity or anti-corruption programmes can also help an SOE in defence of corporate liability. [1] All of these implications of corruption were voiced as a concern by SOEs in this study.

The analysis of this chapter is primarily framed by key elements of integrity and compliance mechanisms and approaches, promoted in the OECD, United Nations Office on Drugs and Crime (UNODC) and World Bank (2013), *Anti-Corruption Ethics and Compliance Handbook for Business*. It benefits from internationally agreed upon standards issued by the OECD. Particularly pertinent key instruments for SOEs and for the state as owner are provided in Box 2.1.

Box 2.1. Overview of existing OECD sources on promoting integrity in the public and private spheres

Convention on Combating Bribery of Foreign Public Officials in International Business Transactions (1997) (*Implementing body: Working Group on Bribery in International Business Transactions*)

Recommendation of the Council on Improving Ethical Conduct in the Public Service Including Principles for Managing Ethics in the Public Service (1998), (*Implementing body: Public Management Committee now called Public Governance Committee*)

Recommendation of the Council on OECD Guidelines for Managing Conflict of Interest in the Public Service (2003), (*Implementing body: Public Management Committee now called Public Governance Committee*)

OECD Principles for Transparency and Integrity in Lobbying (2010) (*Implementing body: Corporate Governance Committee*)

Recommendation of the Council for Further Combating Bribery of Foreign Public Officials in International Business Transactions (2009, including its Annex II: Good Practice Guidance on Internal Controls, Ethics and Compliance added in 2010) (*Implementing body: Working Group on Bribery in International Business Transactions*)

Guidelines for Multinational Enterprises (2011) (*Implementing body: Investment Committee*)

Recommendation on Fighting Bid Rigging in Public Procurement (2012) (*Implementing body: Competition Committee*)

Recommendation of the Council on Public Procurement (2015) *(Implementing body: Public Governance Committee)*

G20/OECD Principles of Corporate Governance (2015) (*Implementing body: Corporate Governance Committee*)

Recommendation of the Council for Development Co-operation Actors on Managing Risks of Corruption (update to the DAC Recommendation on Anti-Corruption Proposals for Bilateral Aid Procurement of 1996) (*Implementing bodies: Development Assistance Committee and the Working Group on Bribery in International Business Transactions)*

Recommendation of the Council on Integrity in Public Procurement (2016) (*Implementing body: Public Governance Committee*)

Recommendation of the Council on Public Integrity (2017) (*Implementing body: Public Governance Committee*)

Tackling obstacles to integrity

The OECD survey of SOEs tracked challenges to improving integrity in their companies. Obstacles to integrity, when aggregated at the country level, are moderately and negatively associated with country scores on the World Justice Project's Rule of Law Index. In other words, companies in countries that rank higher on the Rule of Law Index (that is, better rule of law) consider the obstacles to integrity facing their company as lower. This suggests that respondents' assessments of the obstacles to integrity are somewhat influenced by exogenous factors that form the components of the Rule of Law Index, including, but not limited to: the country's constraints on government powers, absence of corruption, regulatory enforcement and criminal and civil justice. [2] This moderate negative correlation may indicate that SOE assessments of obstacles may be a useful proxy for pinpointing where improvements can be concretely made within SOEs and in their operating environment.

Table 2.1 shows how SOE respondents assess obstacles to integrity in their company. Overall, respondents do not report facing grave obstacles – with respondents rating most obstacles presented to them (Annex 2.A1) as "does not exist", exists but "not at all an obstacle" or "somewhat an obstacle". While respondents do not differ in how they rate the severity of obstacles to their company, they do differ in terms of the types of obstacles they consider their company to face.

Table 2.1. Assessments of obstacles to integrity by respondent characteristics

Aggregated responses to: "In your opinion, to what degree does each factor pose as an obstacle to effectively promoting integrity and preventing corruption in, or involving, your company?"

	% of respondents that say risks of corruption or other irregular practices materialised in the last three years	Type of obstacles to integrity respondent company faces
Overall sample average	**42%**	1. A lack of a culture of integrity in the political and public sector 2. A lack of awareness among employees of the need for, or priority placed on, integrity 3. Opportunistic behaviour of individuals
Respondent's position / role in the company		
Board member	43%	1. A lack of a culture of integrity in the political and public sector 2. Opportunistic behaviour of individuals 3. A lack of awareness among employees of the need for, or priority placed on, integrity
Executive Management	36%	1. A lack of a culture of integrity in the political and public sector 2. A lack of awareness among employees of the need for, or priority placed on, integrity 3. Opportunistic behaviour of individuals
Heads of the corporate audit, compliance or legal functions	45%	1. A lack of a culture of integrity in the political and public sector 2. A lack of awareness among employees of the need for, or priority placed on, integrity 3. Opportunistic behaviour of individuals
Other	46%	1. A lack of a culture of integrity in the political and public sector 2. A lack of awareness among employees of the need for, or priority placed on, integrity 3. Opportunistic behaviour of individuals
Respondent's company: sector		
Agriculture and Fishing	36%	1. A lack of a culture of integrity in the political and public sector 2. Opportunistic behaviour of individuals 3. Inadequate remuneration/compensation
Banking and related financial services	33%	1. A lack of a culture of integrity in the political and public sector 2. A lack of awareness among employees of the need for, or priority placed on, integrity 3. Inadequate financial or human resources to invest in integrity and prevent corruption
Energy (i.e. electricity generation and supply)	42%	1. A lack of a culture of integrity in the political and public sector 2. A lack of awareness among employees of the need for, or priority placed on, integrity 3. Opportunistic behaviour of individuals
Information and Communication Technology (ICT)	33%	1. A lack of awareness among employees of the need for, or priority placed on, integrity 2. Perceived likelihood of getting caught is low 3. Opportunistic behaviour of individuals
Mining	50%	1. Ineffective channels for whistleblowing / reporting misconduct 2. A lack of a culture of integrity in the political and public sector 3. Inadequate resources
Oil and Gas	63%	1. Overly complex or burdensome legal requirements 2. A lack of awareness among employees of the need for, or priority placed on, integrity 3. Opportunistic behaviour of individuals
Postal	45%	1. A lack of a culture of integrity in the political and public sector 2. Loyalty to company 3. A lack of awareness among employees of the need for, or priority placed on, integrity

	% of respondents that say risks of corruption or other irregular practices materialised in the last three years	Type of obstacles to integrity respondent company faces
Transportation and Logistics	42%	1. A lack of awareness among employees of the need for, or priority placed on, integrity 2. Opportunistic behaviour of individuals 3. Perceived likelihood of getting caught is low
Respondent's company objectives		
Entirely commercial	49%	1. A lack of awareness among employees of the need for, or priority placed on, integrity 2. A lack of awareness of legal requirements 3. Inadequate financial or human resources to invest in integrity and prevent corruption
Mixed objectives (commercial with public policy)	36%	1. A lack of a culture of integrity in the political and public sector 2. A lack of awareness among employees of the need for, or priority placed on, integrity 3. Opportunistic behaviour of individuals
Respondent's status as a public official		
Public official	42%	1. A lack of a culture of integrity in the political and public sector 2. A lack of awareness among employees of the need for, or priority placed on, integrity 3. Opportunistic behaviour of individuals
Not a public official	42%	1. A lack of awareness among employees of the need for, or priority placed on, integrity 2. A lack of a culture of integrity in the political and public sector 3. Opportunistic behaviour of individuals

Note: Ranking of individuals' responses to "In your opinion, to what degree does each factor pose as an obstacle to effectively promoting integrity and preventing corruption in, or involving, your company?", ranging from "NA/does not exist in my company" to "very much an obstacle". The risks listed in column 3 are ranked in terms of their rating, and in some cases were equally rated.
Source: OECD 2017 Survey of anti-corruption and integrity in SOEs.

Table 2.2. Top obstacles to integrity: Based on previous experiences with corruption and irregular practices

Top five obstacles to integrity in respondents' companies	
Respondents that witnessed corruption or other irregular practices transpire	Respondents that did not witness corruption or other irregular practices transpire
1. A lack of a culture of integrity in the political and public sector	1. A lack of a culture of integrity in the political and public sector
2. A lack of awareness among employees of the need for, or priority to be placed on, integrity	2. A lack of awareness among employees of the need for, or priority placed on, integrity
3. Opportunistic behaviour of individuals	3. A lack of awareness of legal requirements
4. Perceived likelihood of getting caught is low	4. Opportunistic behaviour of individuals
5. A lack of awareness of legal requirements	5. Overly complex or burdensome legal requirements

Note: Ranking of obstacles to integrity by respondents that responded affirmatively and negatively to "in your assessment, did any of the [listed] risks materialise into activities/actions in the last three years in (or involving) your company?" ranked based on an index from 0 to 3, whereby 0 is "NA/does not exist" to 3 is "very much an obstacle".
Source: OECD 2017 Survey of anti-corruption and integrity in SOEs.

Respondents also report different obstacles as a threat to integrity if they report to have witnessed corrupt or other irregular practices transpire in their company in the last three years (Table 2.2). Those that perceived witnessing corruption or irregularities in their company saw opportunistic behaviour of individuals as an obstacle to their company's integrity, as well as the perception that the likelihood of being caught is low. Those who report that they have not witnessed corruption transpire see their biggest challenge as a lack of awareness. This could suggest that reported corruption or irregular practices in companies in the sample may be a result of opportunistic behaviour that circumvents rules, rather than ignorance to the rules.

The SOE Guidelines recommend that SOEs adhere as closely as possible to corporate practices and the best international standards. Table 2.3 shows the top obstacles to integrity for the participating SOEs in column A. For comparison, column B shows internationally recognised key elements of effective compliance and integrity approaches in business. The key elements are rooted in those found across more than ten international instruments, summarised in Annex 2.A1, as captured in the OECD, UNODC, World Bank (2013) *Anti-Corruption, Ethics and Compliance Handbook for Integrity*. While directed at the private sector, these elements are similar to those required by governments to ensure integrity and mitigate fraud, waste and abuse in the public sector. Elements appear in OECD's Recommendation for Public Integrity, as well as SOE-specific guidance such as Transparency International's 2017 "10 Anti-Corruption Principles for State-Owned Enterprises".

The obstacles in Table 2.3 (column A) may represent weaknesses or blind spots to the SOE that could leave them exposed to corruption or other irregular practices by corporate insiders or outsiders. The sub-sections below propose elements of an overall corporate approach that may be instrumental in overcoming such obstacles, allowing SOEs to meet international standards for effective integrity, compliance and anti-corruption for state owned and non-state owned companies (column B).

Table 2.3. Counteracting perceived obstacles to integrity in state-owned enterprises

A. What are the obstacles to integrity?	B. How can SOEs overcome obstacles to integrity?
A. Top ten obstacles to integrity in SOEs (as rated by 347 SOE respondents)	B. Key elements of effective integrity, anti-corruption or compliance mechanisms or programmes
1. A lack of a culture of integrity in the political and public sector 2. A lack of awareness among employees of the need for, or priority placed on, integrity 3. Opportunistic behaviour of individuals 4. A lack of awareness of legal requirements 5. Perceived likelihood of getting caught is low 6. A lack of a culture of integrity in the company 7. Overly complex or burdensome legal requirements 8. Inadequate financial or human resources to invest in integrity and prevent corruption 9. Ineffective internal control or risk management 10. Ineffective channels for whistleblowing / reporting misconduct	1. A culture of integrity through tone at the top and mechanisms to operationalise it 2. Autonomy and resources for integrity mechanisms 3. Risk Management and assessment 4. Standards of conduct/policies and internal controls 5. Third party management and due diligence 6. Education and training on anti-corruption and integrity 7. Disclosure, monitoring and auditing 8. Detection, advice and complaints channels 9. Incentives for integrity 10. Investigation, response and improvement

Note: The ten obstacles were ranked out of a list of 24 obstacles put forth to SOE respondents, found in the Annex of Chapter 2, and generated based on an index constructed from 0 to 3 (from "does not exist in my company" to "very much an obstacle")
Source: Column A: OECD 2017 Survey of anti-corruption and integrity in SOEs. Column B: Adapted from sections of, and international principles captured in, OECD, UNODC and World Bank (2013), *Anti-Corruption Ethics and Compliance Handbook for Business*, www.oecd.org/corruption/anticorruption-ethics-and-compliance-handbook-for-business.htm.

Box 2.2 elaborates on how weaknesses such as those identified by SOE respondents have exposed organisations to fraud, as illustrating the link between obstacles and misconduct. The study in Box 2.2 demonstrates that fraud resulted from not only an absence of appropriate controls or review, but from override of existing controls.

Box 2.2. Primary control weaknesses observed in cases of occupational fraud

A study on victims of occupational fraud found cited the weaknesses below that exposed their organisation to fraud cases – 37.4% of which also overlapped with corruption.

As such, the findings can be instructive for SOEs seeking to mitigate corruption by establishing necessary safeguards and filling in vulnerabilities:

1. Lack of internal controls (internal controls discussed under "key element 4")
2. Override of existing internal controls (internal controls discussed under "key element 4")
3. Lack of management review (monitoring is covered under "key element 7")
4. Poor tone at the top ("tone at the top" discussed under "key element 1")
5. Lack of competent personnel in oversight roles (capacity and resourcing for oversight discussed in section "key element 2")
6. Lack of independent checks and audits (monitoring an auditing discussed under "key element 7")
7. Lack of employee fraud education (education and training discussed under "key element 6")
8. Lack of clear lines of authority (authority and autonomy discussed in "key element 2")
9. Lack of reporting mechanisms (detection and advice channels discussed in "key element 8")

Source: Association of Certified Fraud Examiners (ACFE) (2016), *Report to the Nations on Occupational Fraud and Abuse*, 2016 Global Fraud Survey, www.acfe.com/rttn2016/docs/2016-report-to-the-nations.pdf

SOEs' existing approaches to integrity by SOEs are either stratified throughout a company or packaged into a complete integrity, compliance or anti-corruption programme. The particular choice as to whether to create an explicit anti-corruption, compliance or similar "programme" may be delegated through the state-ownership entity's expectations, outlined in the legal and regulatory framework or up to the discretion of the board of executive management of the SOE. Whether or not they are formalised into an explicit "programme", SOEs should still strive to implement key elements of a good practice programme taking into account SOE capacity, size, risk profile and risk tolerance levels.

Element 1: A "tone at the top" and a plan for operationalisation

Similar to privately incorporated SOEs, SOE boards and executive management have the job of operationalising the requirements found in the legal framework that support prevention, detection, and response to corruption and other irregular practices. Particularly for SOEs, the state is also instrumental in setting a tone – a "tone from the top" – through the establishment and communication of expectations.

Instilling a culture of integrity is broader than compliance. Compliance can, and is often, treated narrowly as the adherence to relevant rules that exist. A culture of integrity – promoting "doing the right thing" – extends beyond seeking the letter of the law. The state's encouragement towards integrity should be spelled out clearly in the state's expectations to avoid additional or ad-hoc burdens on SOEs, or to avoid it being used as a cover for intervention in the operations of SOEs.

SOEs may choose or be required to tailor and implement explicit state expectations regarding anti-corruption and integrity in SOEs that may be more or less stringent than those applying to privately incorporated companies. The SOE Guidelines recommend that SOEs adhere, as closely as possible, to corporate practices and the best international standards. In some countries, anti-corruption and integrity-related mechanisms are implemented in line with requirements for public sector entities. In one UK company, state requirements to adopt relevant codes is placed on all government departments and agencies although each body is free to establish the shape, size, content and method of communication (and associated methods of control). In other cases, SOEs may be limited in their approach to integrity by the state's requirements, or lack thereof.

A tone from the top and promotion of integrity in SOEs could be improved, as almost half (47%) of SOEs lost annual corporate profits to corruption or other rule-breaking at 3% on average in the last year.[3] Results show that 25% of heads of the corporate audit, compliance or legal functions, and 18% of executive management board members reported that "unsupportive leadership from the board and management" is at least "somewhat an obstacle to integrity in their company." The variance in opinion by respondent position points to a respondent bias. Further, the following obstacles were highlighted amongst the greatest obstacles by SOE respondents:

- A lack of awareness among employees of the need for, or priority placed on, integrity.
- Existence of behavioural issues, such as opportunistic behaviour of individuals, a perception that the likelihood of getting caught is low, or perverse incentives such as pressure to perform or to break the rules.
- A lack of a culture of integrity in the political and public sector. The states' responsibility in this regard is discussed in Chapter 3. SOE leadership is also responsible for insulating its company from any undue influence – state or otherwise.

SOE leadership can tackle such issues by establishing a clear "tone from the top" – a clearly articulated mission statement or visible corporate policy that explicitly addresses the topic of integrity, ethics or anti-corruption and is integrated into the corporate strategy. Orchestrating a believable approach to combatting corruption and promoting integrity in a company will require bringing leadership onto the same page. Figure 2.1 shows that board members, integrity managers and executive management have different perspectives on the allocation of budget to integrity functions in their company. Fifty-seven percent of board members see it as an asset or investment, higher than integrity managers (52%) and executive management (42%).

A high proportion of companies' existing approaches to integrity and anti-corruption have been self-driven or voluntarily established by leadership. However, the foremost driver of these mechanisms has been to comply with requirements that have been imposed or requested. A majority were also driven to implement such measures for fear of reputational damage. Forty percent of respondents also pointed to a risk of corruption, and a risk of legal enforcement or divestment as a significant impetus for establishing their current approaches. Private sector companies reported, in the 2015 OECD study on Trust in Business, similar reasons for seeking to prevent and address corporate misconduct (OECD, 2015a).

Figure 2.1. Allocation of operational budget to anti-corruption and integrity: Investment or cost?

Responses to the question: "How would you characterise the allocation of operational budget to preventing, detecting and addressing integrity and anti-corruption?"

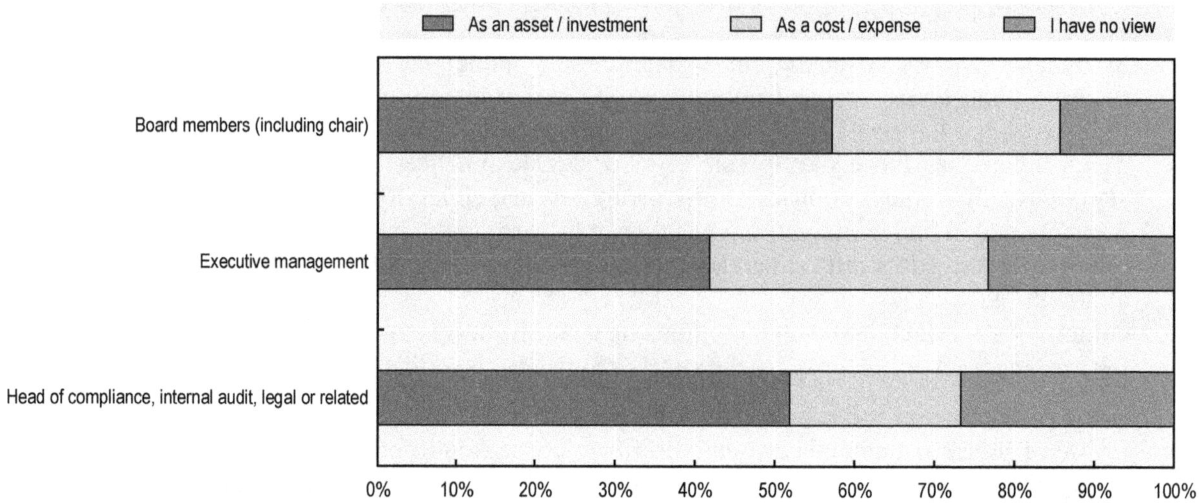

Note: Board members included Chairs and other board members; Executive management included Chief Executive Officers/Presidents/Managing Directors, Chief Financial Officer or similar or other "C-suite" executives; the group of heads of the corporate audit, compliance or legal functions also included Chief Risk and Chief Sustainability Officers.
Source: OECD 2017 Survey of anti-corruption and integrity in SOEs

A culture of integrity importantly includes the understanding throughout the ranks of the company that anti-corruption and integrity initiatives are part of the broader strategy towards the achievement of SOE goals. Where they are seen as a drain on the company, there is scope to better link them to strategic objectives and to disseminate the understanding of their importance for achievement of goals and mitigation of reputational damage and losses to waste and abuse.

The tone from the top should include clear instruction on how such anti-corruption and integrity efforts will be operationalised – from prevention, through detection, enforcement and improvement – embodied in codes and standards. The SOE Guidelines state that "boards of SOEs should develop, implement, monitor and communicate internal controls, ethics and compliance programmes or measures, including those which contribute to preventing fraud and corruption. They should be based on country norms, in conformity with international commitments and apply to the SOE and its subsidiaries" (OECD, 2015b). Further, one key step of Enterprise Risk Management is that management selects a set of actions to align risks with the entity's risk tolerances and risk appetite (the Committee of Sponsoring Organizations of the Treadway Commission [COSO], 2017).

In some countries, a specific anti-corruption, compliance or integrity programme is established, while in others the approach to integrity is captured in a specific code of conduct, or similar, backed by relevant controls. An SOEs' approach may be dictated or simply recommended by the state ownership entity, or at the full discretion of the board and executive management. Relevant company examples provided in the OECD 2017 survey of anti-corruption and integrity in SOEs include:

- One Finnish company that has established a "Total Compliance" programme which covers key areas of regulatory compliance and business ethics. It is managed with risk-based prioritisation. Internal Controls are integral part of the Total Compliance and both the Group Compliance Officer and the Head of Internal Controls report to the General Counsel independently of the business. The Code of Conduct and compliance topics and instructions are communicated through internal and external communication channels. Alignment is enforced by top management with their full commitment.
- An Italian SOE's board that deliberated in 2016 the adoption of an integrated anti-corruption system that will be composed by the existing Compliance Model according Legislative Decree 231/2001 and an Anti-Corruption Model, to be created after the deliberation of the Anticorruption Policy. The goal is to cover a larger spectrum of illicit practices not considered by specific company legislation.
- A Norwegian company has a formal compliance programme in place, as required. This is based on a range of international standards, with particular reference being made to the guidelines issued for the UK Bribery Act and the recently approved International Organization for Standardization (ISO) standard on anti-bribery management systems. The programme includes the following key elements: tone from the top; risk assessment; proportionate procedures; due diligence; training and communication; monitoring and review. A corporate compliance unit has been established, and there is a network of compliance resources in all business and staff areas. The programme is regularly reviewed and audited, including by external auditors.
- A Costa Rican company that is bound by the Manual of Standards of Internal Control for the Public Sector (Standard 2.3.1), on the "Formal Factors of Institutional Ethics", which requires establishment of formal factors to promote and strengthen institutional ethics, including at least those relating to: a) the formal statement of vision, mission, and institutional values; b) a code of ethics or similar; c) indicators that allow for following the institutional ethical culture and the effectiveness of the formal elements for its strengthening and; d) an implementation strategy to formalise commitments, policies and regular programs to evaluate, update, and renew the institution's commitment to ethics.

SOE leadership will also need to demonstrate a commitment to anti-corruption and integrity through support to related processes and through adherence to the highest standards. Naturally, it would follow that leadership should not under any circumstance be involved in corruption or other irregular practices. Yet, as shown in Chapter 1, 25% of respondents witnessed corruption or other irregular practices involving senior management and 16% involving board members.

Leadership should effectively execute its own duties regarding anti-corruption and integrity. In one country, the state ownership entity stressed that boards of directors need to think strategically, while considering risks involved in the planning process that include corruption risks. In spite of the fact that these SOEs are obliged to have a risk matrix as a tool for monitoring this type of risk, boards of directors rarely discuss it. Oversight and monitoring of integrity and anti-corruption programmes or mechanisms in a company is discussed further below.

SOE leadership and state ownership entities can consider assessing the adequacy and effectiveness of their "tone from the top" and their ability to build a culture of integrity in their company. Box 2.3 provides example questions that companies may use to self-assess the adequacy of their tone from the top.

Box 2.3. Key questions to assess effectiveness of companies' tone from the top regarding anti-corruption and integrity

- Is active commitment and visible support given by management?
- Has there been clear, practical and accessible communication of the compliance programme and standards to employees?
- Has management established a trust-based organisational culture, adopting the principles of openness and transparency?
- Are appropriate levels of oversight of subsidiary operations established?
- What structures and processes are in place to enable oversight?
- What information is required by management in real-time or periodic reporting?

Source: OECD, UNODC and the World Bank, Anti-Corruption Ethics and Compliance Handbook for Business (2013), www.oecd.org/corruption/anti-corruption-ethics-and-compliance-handbook-for-business.htm.

Element 2: Autonomy and resourcing of integrity mechanisms and programmes

Departments with a primary responsibility for integrity should have sufficient autonomy, stature, capacity, and resources to execute accordingly. This section focuses on autonomy of the integrity function, while elaboration on the importance of board autonomy is found in Chapter 3.

Resourcing of corruption prevention and detection

Eighty-one percent of participating companies that invest in integrity allocate on average 1.5% of the operational budget to preventing, detecting and addressing corruption and breaches of integrity. Yet "inadequate financial or human resources to invest in integrity and prevent corruption" is considered at least "somewhat of an obstacle" for 40% of SOE respondents. This figure is slightly lower than in private sector companies, as reported by OECD's *Corporate Governance and Business Integrity: A stocktaking of Corporate Practices* (2015a), where 26% of respondents felt that they had inadequate financial and human resources to establish an effective integrity policy (OECD, 2015a).

SOEs see allocation of financial and human resources to integrity as more of a burden than the private sector. Overall, 50% of SOE respondents saw such allocation of budget as an investment or asset and 27% saw it as a cost or expense. *Corporate Governance and Business Integrity* showed that 60% of companies felt such allocation was an investment and only 18% as a cost (OECD, 2015a).

Autonomy of SOE leadership and integrity functions

A distinct difference between SOEs and private companies is the need for board autonomy from the state owner – insulating the board from direction by state representatives that is misaligned with the role of the state as owner as elaborated in the SOE Guidelines. Board autonomy is discussed in Chapter 3.

Figure 2.2. Main activities undertaken by the integrity function

Non-exhaustive list of activities undertaken by SOE units/functions assigned significant responsibility for integrity, according to individual respondents

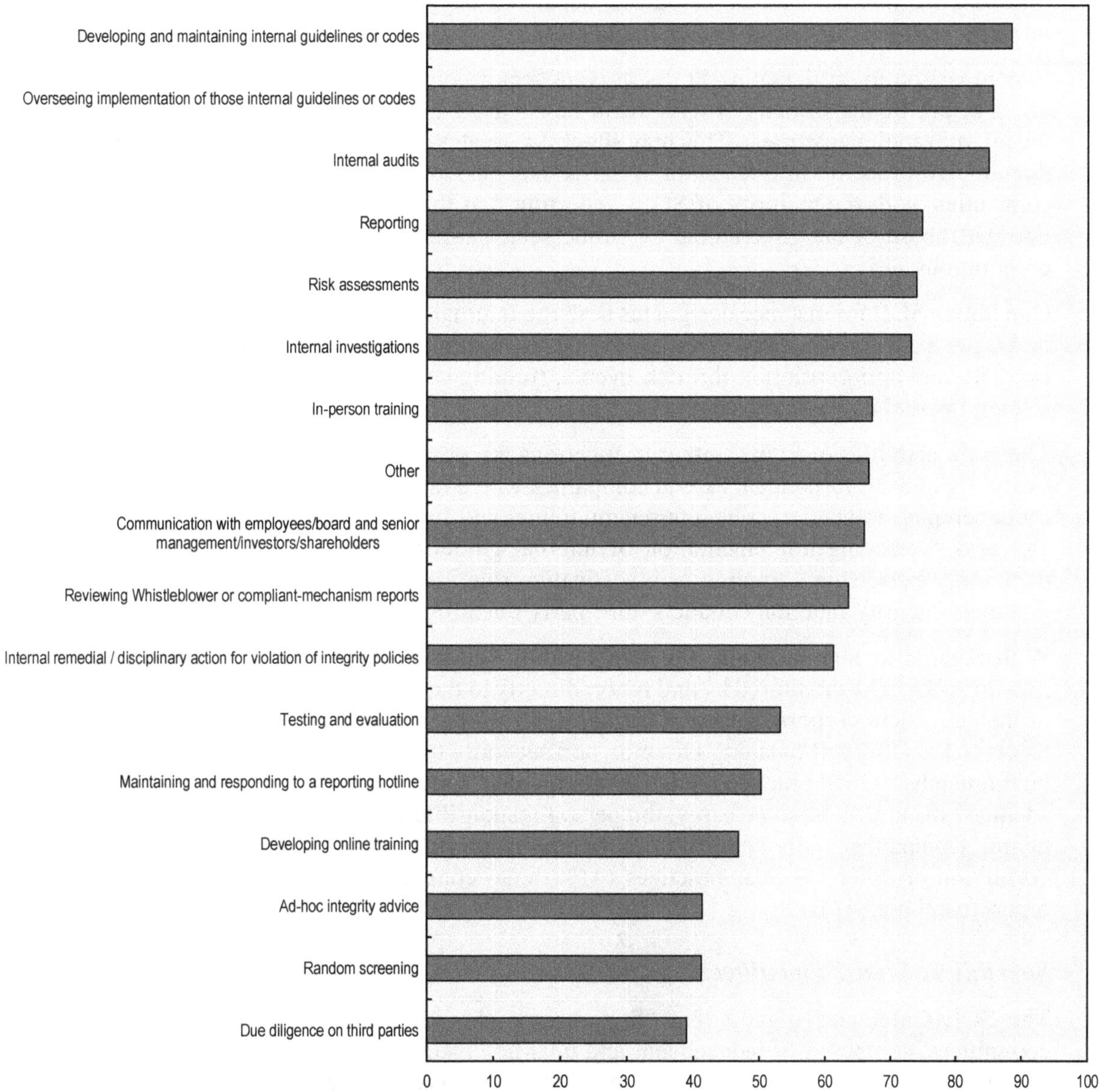

Note: Based on 347 individual responses. Other was not specified.
Source: OECD 2017 Survey of Anti-Corruption and integrity in SOEs.

Autonomy is also needed for those responsible for integrity to exercise their role objectively and in accordance with the best interests of the company and with international standards. In cases where executive management and those involved in integrity functions, such as the CEO or internal audit, are appointed by the state, this is a direct challenge to the independence and autonomy that the integrity functions and the SOE rely on to mitigate undue influence and to manage conflicts of interest.

The internal audit department is most commonly assigned significant responsibility for promoting and overseeing integrity or integrity policies in participating SOEs (relating to risk, controls, compliance ethics or anti-corruption), but often shares the responsibility with others. Legal departments are the second group most often given this responsibility, followed by internal human resources departments. In most SOEs responsibility for integrity is shared between more than one unit.

In comparison to participating SOEs, private sector companies tend to organise integrity under a specific department, or with the in-house legal department, more often than within the internal audit department. This may suggest a greater reliance on internal audit by SOEs than in private sector. Internal audit in SOEs may also look different than in private sector companies, with the majority of SOEs reporting that their internal audit functions are in line with those of the government or public sector entities rather than in line with other corporations.

One Italian SOE for instance designates both the internal audit department and supervisory body, pursuant to Legislative Decree 231/01, as responsible for promoting and ensuring integrity and anti-corruption through events, training sessions, monitoring activities and issuing internal disciplinary sanctions.

The main activities of SOEs' integrity functions are provided in Figure 2.2, showing that over 88% of SOE respondents are in companies where the integrity function is responsible for developing and maintaining internal guidelines and controls, undertaking internal audits and also overseeing implementation of internal guidelines and controls. They are also commonly exercising a training or investigative role. Less than 40% of respondents said that their integrity function conducts third-party due diligence.

With regards to internal audit, the OECD SOE Guidelines state that the internal audit function should be monitored by and report directly to the board, and to the audit committee or the equivalent corporate organ. The majority of units responsible for integrity in SOEs report to the CEO or Managing Director, and secondly to the chair of the board or another board member. Good practice holds that companies' senior corporate officers should have adequate resources. In some cases, the person responsible for the integrity unit sits on the board. Companies with opportunities to report to both have witnessed slightly less corruption or other irregular practices (41%) than companies whose integrity functions report to neither (47%).

Specialised board committees

The SOE Guidelines suggest that "SOE boards should consider setting up specialised committees, composed of independent and qualified members, to support the full board in performing its functions, particularly in respect to audit, risk management and remuneration".

The most common specialised committees are audit committees (84% of respondents report their SOE has one). More than half of respondents' companies have a risk management committee, and less than half (43%) have a remuneration committee. Less common, yet in roughly one third of companies, are specialised committees for ethics (39%), compliance (34%) or public procurement (28%).

Respondents in companies with specialised committees in audit, risk management, remuneration and public procurement rate the likelihood of corruption as lower than those whose companies do not have the aforementioned committees. Risk management committees on the board are additionally associated with a lower rate of witnessing corruption than those without risk management committees.

Box 2.4. Key questions to assess adequacy of autonomy and resourcing for anti-corruption and integrity

Autonomy – Have the compliance and relevant control functions had direct reporting lines to anyone on the board of directors? How often do they meet with the board of directors? Are members of the senior management present for these meetings? Who reviewed the performance of the compliance function and what was the review process? Who determines the compensation, bonuses, raises, hiring, or termination of compliance officers? Do the compliance and relevant control personnel in the field have reporting lines to headquarters? If not, how has the company ensured their independence?

Empowerment – Have there been specific instances where compliance raised concerns or objections in the area in which the wrongdoing occurred? How has the company responded to such compliance concerns? Have there been specific transactions or deals that were stopped, modified, or more closely examined as a result of compliance concerns?

Stature – How has the compliance function compared with other strategic functions in the company in terms of stature, compensation levels, rank/title, reporting line, resources, and access to key decision makers? What has been the turnover rate for compliance and relevant control function personnel? What role has compliance played in the company's strategic and operational decisions?

Experience and Qualifications – Have the compliance and control personnel had the appropriate experience and qualifications for their roles and responsibilities?

Funding and Resources – How have decisions been made about the allocation of personnel and resources for the compliance and relevant control functions in light of the company's risk profile? Have there been times when requests for resources by the compliance and relevant control functions have been denied? If so, how have those decisions been made?

Outsourced Compliance Functions – Has the company outsourced all or parts of its compliance functions to an external firm or consultant? What has been the rationale for doing so? Who has been involved in the decision to outsource? How has that process been managed (including who oversaw and/or liaised with the external firm/consultant)? What access level does the external firm or consultant have to company information? How has the effectiveness of the outsourced process been assessed?

Source: Department of Justice, United States (2017), "Evaluation of Corporate Compliance Programs", www.justice.gov/criminal-fraud/page/file/937501/download.

In a few cases, specialised committees may exist external to the board, at the executive management level. This is the case in one Norwegian Company, which has compliance and risk committees that are executive management committees, or in one Italian company that has *Control and Risk, Compensation and Sustainability and Scenarios Committees* external to the board.

Specialised committees should have adequate autonomy and distance from executive management and employees in order to provide adequate oversight. This is particularly challenging when such committees are established at the executive management level.

Of high importance is the adequacy of the capacity and skills set of those responsible for integrity – including those on specialised committees – and the stature and authority of the departments in the company. Box 2.4 provides suggested questions that may be used by the US Department of Justice, particularly pertaining to the adequacy of autonomy and resourcing of those responsible for integrity in face of corruption suspicions. They are not meant to be used as a specific checklist, but as a guide for companies' self-evaluation and reflection.

Element 3: Risk assessment and management

Good practice as laid out by international standard setters, such as the Committee of Sponsoring Organizations of the Treadway Commission (COSO, 2017), promote integration of risk management into strategic and operational processes of the company. Yet too often risks, let alone corruption risks, are treated separately from decision-making processes. Those companies that do explicitly treat corruption risks do so as part of compliance risks, and fewer as strategic, operational or financial risks. In addition to the four categories shown in Table 2.4, corruption risks are treated as completely separate in 3% of companies. Ten percent of companies in the sample do not treat corruption risks explicitly.

Risk assessments aimed specifically at identifying, analysing and prioritising corruption risks are done on an annual basis in 79% of participating companies (Figure 2.3). SOE respondents in companies that never conduct corruption-related risk assessments or that conduct them every two-to-three years reported witnessing corruption and other irregular practices more often than companies that conduct annual risk assessments. They also consider corruption risks as more likely to transpire and that mechanisms for prevention and detection (internal controls, risk management, internal audit and reporting) are more of a challenge to their company's integrity.

Table 2.4. Categorisation of corruption risks in state-owned enterprises

Risk category	Example business objectives by risk category	Examples of risk factors ("a condition that is associated with a higher probability of risk consequences")	% SOEs subsuming anti-corruption and integrity risks into each category
Strategic risk factors	Protect the brand from reputational damage	Competitive and economic environment; impact on stakeholder value	18%
Operational risk factors	Enhance likelihood of company success by providing exceptional services	Dependence on strategic partners; management competence; workforce skill and competence	17%
Financial risk factors	Strengthen the probity and accuracy of annual accounts	Susceptibility to fraud; complexity of transactions; recent cash flow trends	6%
Compliance risk factors	Comply with local, domestic and international laws	Extent of regulatory influence on operations; tone at the top by leadership; magnitude of fines or other penalties.	38%

Note: The percentage of companies is based on responses from valid responses of 169 companies in response to "Under which category of risks does your company explicitly categorise integrity or anti-corruption risks, if at all". Five percent of SOEs report to categories corruption risks in multiple ways, and 3% said they are treated in another way.

Source: Categories adopted from Georgetown University (2017), Impact, Likelihood and Velocity, https://riskmanagement.georgetown.edu/RiskAssessmentMeasures; and OECD 2017 Survey of anti-corruption and integrity in SOEs.

Figure 2.3. Regularity of corruption-related risk assessments in state-owned enterprises

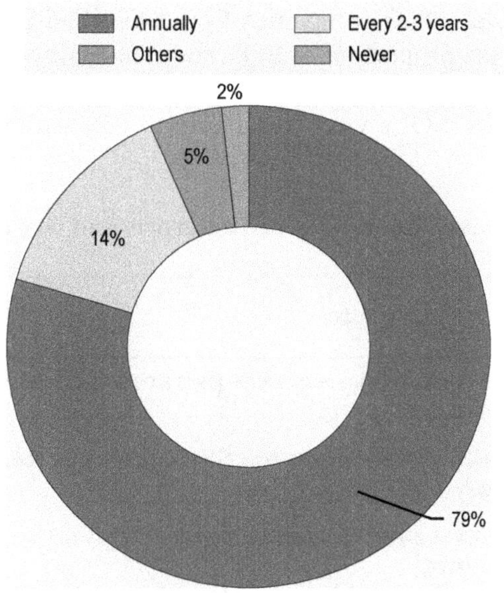

Note: Based on 213 company responses to: "how often does your company generally conduct risk assessments aimed specifically at identifying, analysing and prioritising corruption risks?"
Source: OECD 2017 Survey of anti-corruption and integrity in SOEs.

Boards should be duly informed about material risks to the company. Table 2.5 shows that boards of participating SOEs are more likely to receive integrity-related findings than are executive management. This is not surprising, but it raises the question as to whether management should be more informed about the risks to the company. As mentioned above, these two groups perceive risks differently from each other and from those who prepare and present the reports or findings.

Table 2.5. To whom are integrity-related recommendations and findings presented?

Of 347 responses to the question "Please select the following integrity-related findings/recommendations/assessments that are brought to the attention of your company's leadership."

Type of recommendations, findings or assessments	Percentage of respondents whose companies present such findings to the:	
	Board	Executive Management
Findings of risk assessments that point to integrity or corruption risks	**71**	66
Internal audit findings/recommendations	**83**	71
External audit findings/recommendations	**83**	66
Recommendations from integrity functions	49	**58**
Evaluations of internal controls (that may be separate from internal audits)	32	**36**
Reports or claims of irregular practices or corruption made through reporting channels	**59**	57

Source: OECD 2017 Survey of anti-corruption and integrity in SOEs.

SOE boards could use risk assessment results to better insulate the company from the risks identified in this report. Sound risk assessments should underpin internal controls and integrity mechanisms or programmes that are proportionate to risks. They should be used to improve on a continuous basis thereafter.

Some SOEs seek to insulate their companies from identified potential or real corruption risks. Table 2.6 outlines the proportion of SOE and non-SOE companies that have ceased business operations, taken internal remedial action or that have revised business projects in the face of corruption risks. SOEs were less likely to take action than non SOEs in each category.

Table 2.6. Actions taken by state-owned enterprises in face of corruption risks

Action	SOEs	Non SOEs
Respondents said their companies have ceased business operations in a particular jurisdiction because of the integrity or corruption risks involved	12%	39%
Respondents that said their companies have taken internal remedial/disciplinary action following violation of your organisation's integrity or anti-corruption policies.	46%	70%
Respondents said their companies have substantially revised at least one business project because of the corruption and integrity risk(s) involved.	30%	66%

Note: This analysis is done on 261 individual responses – not by company. Broad comparisons made with a survey of non-SOEs where the number of respondents was 57.
Source: OECD 2017 Survey of anti-corruption and integrity in SOEs; OECD (2015), Trust and Business.

Inspiration for risk practices may be drawn from a UK company that has a risk management framework with seven *Level 1 Risk Categories*, each of which is used by the Board to set its risk appetite (encompassed in the "Risk Appetite Statements"): strategic and business risk, market risk, credit & investment risk, operational risk (including financial crime), information risk, legal & compliance risk and reputational risk. These are cascaded to 27 *Level 2 Risk Categories* and used to asses and monitor if the company is managing these risks within the risk appetite. This monitoring includes the use of Key Risk Indicators.

Box 2.5 provides example questions that companies may use to self-assess the adequacy of their risk management, as put forth in the OECD, UNODC and World Bank, *Anti-Corruption Ethics and Compliance Handbook for Business* (2013).

Box 2.5. Key questions for companies to ask about risk assessment

- Who owns the process, and who are the key stakeholders?
- How much time will be invested in the process?
- What type of data should be collected, and how?
- What internal and external resources are needed?
- What framework will be used to document, measure, and manage the corruption risk?

Source: OECD, UNODC and the World Bank, Anti-Corruption Ethics and Compliance Handbook for Business (2013), www.oecd.org/corruption/anti-corruption-ethics-and-compliance-handbook-for-business.htm.

Element 4: Standards of conduct and internal controls

The SOE Guidelines (2015b) recommend that boards of SOEs "should develop, implement, monitor and communicate internal controls, ethics and compliance programmes or measures, including those which contribute to preventing fraud and corruption. They should be based on country norms, in conformity with international commitments and apply to the SOE and its subsidiaries."

Codes and policies

SOEs may be subject to relevant provisions for preventing, detecting and responding to corruption and other irregular practices found in the overarching legal framework. Such requirements are discussed in Chapter 3. SOEs may also be encouraged to adopt soft law instruments or other national or supranational codes that are not formally part of the legal framework. For instance, Codes of Corporate Governance are often applied on a voluntary comply-or-explain basis. While such voluntary codes play an important role in improving corporate governance arrangements, shareholders may be unclear about their status and implementation. Considerations for the state as owner, including to be informed about the existence and implementation of rules and codes, are made in Chapter 3.

Codes of ethics should apply to the SOEs as a whole and to their subsidiaries. They should give clear and detailed guidance as to the expected conduct of all employees and compliance programmes and measures should be established. It is considered good practice for these codes to be developed in a participatory way in order to involve all the employees and stakeholders concerned. These codes should benefit from visible support and commitment by the boards and senior management. SOEs' compliance with codes of ethics should be periodically monitored by their boards (OECD, 2015b).

The legal framework will determine which codes and rules are voluntary or Codes may be required on the basis of internal control laws. One Latin American company's Code of Ethics is required by the Ministry of Public Affairs, while the Code of Conduct is required by relevant Banking Law.

SOEs most often aggregate rules in their standards of codes of conduct, ethics, compliance or other. Codes of conduct should be as comprehensive as possible, particularly where they are considered to be the company's statement on integrity and anti-corruption, as well as integrity-related action plan or programme. In addition, they may cover issues related to human rights and broader corporate social responsibility. Company examples include:

- A Norwegian company's policy for Corporate Social Responsibility (CSR), its Integrity Program and its related "Tool Box" are all established on a voluntarily basis, based on COSO. The company has signed the UN Global Compact and reports according to the principles of the Global Reporting Initiative in its annual Sustainability Report.
- In a Polish SOE, the Code defines the principles to be followed by employees and stakeholders in a comprehensive manner, in particular: transparent HR policy, respect for work and professionalism in carrying out tasks, gifts and invitations, conflicts of interest, environmental performance, fair competition, prevention and the fight against fraud and corruption.
- An Italian company, in accordance with the principle of "zero tolerance" towards corruption expressed in the Code of Ethics, has had an articulated system of rules and controls to prevent corruption-related crimes since 2009 in accordance with applicable anti-corruption provisions of international conventions (including the

United Nations Convention Against Corruption [UNCAC], the Anti-Bribery Convention, the US Foreign Corrupt Practices Act, the UK Bribery Act and Italian Legislative Decree 231/2001).

Internal controls in accordance with state-owned enterprise risk profiles

The SOE Guidelines suggest that boards of SOEs should develop, implement, monitor and communicate internal controls. How the board does so may depend on the level of corporatisation of the company and its functional independence from the state-ownership entity.

International standards hold that effective internal controls should be developed based on results of robust risk assessments. As mentioned above, explicitly treating corruption risks in risk assessments enables SOEs to have a more realistic risk profile and to address them with measured controls.

The one-third of SOE respondents who reported that ineffective internal controls and risk management is at least "somewhat of an obstacle" to integrity in their company, were more likely to see corruption in their company in the last three years compared to those that do not see controls as ineffective (52% versus 35% respectively).

Controls can be improved. SOEs should align, to the extent possible, its practices with listed companies. Regardless of whether aligned with public or private sector, controls could include, amongst others:

- Accurate books and records that document all financial transactions (Partnering Against Corruption: Principles for Countering Bribery, 2004);
- Prohibition of off the books accounts and transactions, non-existent expenditure, entry of liabilities with incorrect identification of objects, use of false documents, the deliberate destruction of books or house documents earlier than foreseen by law (OECD Anti-Bribery Convention, 1997; UNCAC, 2003);[4]
- Financial and organisational checks and balances over the enterprises' accounting and record-keeping practices and other business processes (Transparency International et al. *Business Principles for Countering Bribery*, 2013);
- Vetting current and future employees with any decision-making authority or in a position to influence business results (World Bank Group's *Integrity Compliance Guidelines*, 2010);
- Transparent and multi-step approval and certification processes, including that of decision-making processes, that are appropriate for the value of the transaction and perceived risk of misconduct (World Bank Group's *Integrity Compliance Guidelines*, 2010);
- Appropriate contractual obligations for business partners and third parties (World Bank Group's *Integrity Compliance Guidelines*, 2010). Third party and vendor management that is in line with the SOEs' own integrity and anti-corruption policies (discussed below).

Controls should be supported by the human resources department. One control measure proposed in international guidance is to restrict arrangements with former public officials regarding employment or remunerative arrangements. SOEs' involvement with public officials is more complicated, as many SOE board members or executive management members are themselves considered public officials. The need for merit-based and transparent board nominations procedures are discussed in Chapter 3.

Good practice for listed companies is for internal controls systems to be subject to regular, independent internal and external audits to provide objective assurance and determine the adequacy of controls. The SOE Guidelines also recommend that internal auditors are independent, to ensure an efficient and robust disclosure process and proper internal controls in the broad sense. The data shows that in SOEs with a lack of effectiveness in internal control, there are also greater challenges with effectiveness of internal audit. Improvements to controls and internal audit should thus go hand in hand. Internal audit is discussed further below.

Specific corruption risk areas should be embedded in a company's codes (of ethics, compliance or conduct) and addressed by associated internal controls. Commonly agreed standards hold that companies should target specifically: bribery, including facilitation payments, conflicts of interest, solicitation and extortion, and special types of expenditures (including gifts, hospitality, travel and entertainment, political contributions, and charitable contributions and sponsorships).

The findings in Chapter 1 on key corruption risks specific to SOEs emphasise the need for SOEs to have additional policies in relation to integrity in public procurement, favouritism (nepotism, cronyism and patronage) and interference in decision-making. SOEs have rules in place for some key high-risk areas, but not all. Respondents report that their SOEs have an average of four out of seven key rules in place, and fewer than ten companies had all of the below in place:

- Eight-three percent have rules for conflict of interest.
- Sixty-six percent have rules for public procurement (as procurer of goods and services).
- Sixty percent have rules for charitable contributions and sponsorships.
- Fifty-four percent have rules for asset/income disclosure.
- Forty-nine percent have rules for public procurement (as bidder).
- Forty-two percent have rules for political party financing or engagement. One company commented that political contributions are simply out of the question and that there was no need to have rules.
- Twenty-three percent have rules for lobbying. One company's rules regarding lobbying are included in the civil service code, applicable to the SOE.
- SOEs report additional rules relating to anti-money laundering and counter-terrorist financing, travel and gifts, public official meeting registration, election period rules and community relationships, policies and manuals for Politically Exposed Persons (PEPs),[5] related party transactions, anti-fraud and anti-market abuse policy.

Existing codes, rules and controls should be based on international norms and, to the extent possible, be consistent across countries in order for constructive comparisons and consistent audits to be made across SOEs within a country. The international norms most commonly referred to by SOEs participating in this study include: those of the OECD; the Institute of Internal Auditors (IIA), COSO, ISO (particularly ISO 37001); the UK Bribery Act, the Foreign Corrupt Practices Act (FCPA); the Global Compact Programme, and; the United Nations' Convention Against Corruption, Guiding Principles on Business and Human Rights, Convention on the Rights of the Child and the Convention on the Elimination of all Forms of Discrimination against Women and the Principles for Responsible Investment. Some SOEs draw motivation from international comparisons such as Ethisphere's "World's Most Ethical Companies".[6]

Box 2.6. Monitoring implementation of compliance programmes: A compliance assessment checklist

The *Anti-Corruption Ethics and Compliance Handbook for Business* explains how one UK-based international company uses self-assessment as one way to monitor compliance. When the self-assessment tool is applied to the area of conflicts of interest, the unit head seeks to affirm the following:

I understand the issues surrounding actual, perceived or potential conflicts of interest and I confirm that a process has been implemented within my business unit/division to ensure that situations that might give rise to a conflict of interest are disclosed to the company and managed appropriately by an independent person e.g. staff within the human resources or local compliance officer or legal function.

a. My staff are aware that they must disclose to their department head, the human resources, local compliance officer or legal departments if they own, serve on the board of, or have a substantial interest in, a [company] competitor, supplier or contractor; have a significant personal interest or potential gain in any [company] business transaction; hire or supervise a relative who works for [company], or has the opportunity to place company business with a firm owned or controlled by an [company] employee or his or her family.

b. My staff are aware that taking outside employment or freelancing, accepting gifts/entertainment from suppliers, honoraria or other payments from third parties may give rise to an actual, perceived or potential conflict of interest and that if they are in any doubt they must disclose the circumstances to their department head.

c. Management within my business unit have been given appropriate guidance on conflicts of interest and are aware of the issues that must be reported to the local compliance officer or human resources department.

Source: OECD, United Nations Office on Drugs and Crime (UNODC) and the World Bank, Anti-Corruption Ethics and Compliance Handbook for Business (2013), www.oecd.org/corruption/anti-corruption-ethics-and-compliance-handbook-for-business.htm.

Evidence shows that SOEs must go beyond establishing codes, rules and controls to focus also on their effective dissemination, implementation and enforcement. Almost half of SOE respondents identified a "lack of awareness of legal requirements" as at least "somewhat an obstacle" to integrity. Indeed, a high proportion of respondents within the same company – at the highest echelons of the SOE - could not agree on which rules were in place. In addition, the vast majority of SOEs in the survey have conflict of interest rules (83%), yet the risk of nondeclaration is ranked as one of the highest corruption-related risks for companies in terms of the likelihood of occurrence. Box 2.6 provides questions that SOEs may use to assess the effectiveness of their controls. Mechanisms for detection and response are covered in more detail below.

Element 5: Third party management and due diligence

Like private companies, SOEs must "manage" relationships with third parties – taken broadly to refer to those individuals or companies external to the SOE ranging from vendors or suppliers to civil society organisations – in a way that protects the integrity and reputation of the SOE. The SOE Guidelines (OECD, 2015b) stipulate that:

- When SOEs engage in co-operative projects such as joint ventures and public-private partnerships, the contracting party should ensure that contractual rights are upheld and that disputes are addressed in a timely and objective manner.
- When SOEs engage in co-operative projects with private partners, care should be taken to uphold the contractual rights of all parties and to ensure effective redress and/or dispute resolution mechanisms. Relevant other OECD recommendations should be observed, in particular the OECD Principles for Public Governance of Public-Private Partnerships as well as, in the relevant sectors, the OECD Principles for Private Sector Participation in Infrastructure.
- Listed or large SOEs should report on stakeholder relations, including where relevant and feasible with regard to labour, creditors and affected communities.

Other international guidance suggests that third-party management includes the application of anti-corruption measures or programmes to the enterprise's partners and due diligence in the selection and maintenance of business interaction. The G20 High-Level Principles on Private Sector Transparency and Integrity call for businesses to conduct appropriate due diligence and to ensure that subsidiaries, including affiliates over whom they have effective control, have internal controls and ethics and compliance measures commensurate with the risks they face. Transparency International's "10 Anti-Corruption Principles for State-Owned Enterprises" calls for SOEs to "manage relationships with third parties to ensure they perform to an anti-corruption standard equivalent to that of the SOE" (TI, 2017).

The following list of tools used to manage third parties are synthesised from the practices of SOEs participating in the study. SOEs may wish to review them for the comprehensiveness of their own company approach:

- Pre-screening and ex ante risk assessment of third parties and proposals:
    - seeking out fair trade partners when possible, as is done by a company in Poland
    - screening, audits or risk assessments of third parties, as is done in a Norwegian company:
        - analysis of legal, financial and corporate background of contractors
        - cross-checking owners, directors and representatives, and comparing them and affiliates in anti-money laundering and anti-terrorist financing, or bribery, databases
        - sending a questionnaire to new supplier candidates
        - "Know Your Customer" software used in Finnish companies for procurement processes
        - using open sources and dedicated IT tools managed by the security unit, as well due diligence carried out by other business units for specific activities at risk
- risk assessment of proposals
- system support and coordination of risk maps between different functions as is done in Sweden
- independent professional advice may be secured on an as required basis, as is done in New Zealand.

- "Integrity agreements", integrity pacts,7 or integrity or anti-corruption clauses built into contracts. Agreement templates contain anti-bribery and corruption provisions in Finland. In Italy, anti-corruption addendums are added to the contracts that third parties have to accept and sign.
- Code of Conduct attached to supplier agreements or as part of employees' working contracts.
- Using certifying business coalitions or collective engagement with governments or others (including civil society), as is done in Latvia and Mexico. Collective action through informal compliance roundtables with representatives of external companies. Regular contact with public authorities, in trade compliance matters as is done in Sweden.
- Compliance and ethics training and discussions to selected important third parties to clearly explain the company's expectations on ethics and compliance, integrity and anti-corruption.
- Setting related controls for approvals and payments, including checks and balances, procedures to approve contracts and payments to suppliers based on a system of multiple authorisers and matrix of agents based on double signature; authority limits and delegations rules; establishing thresholds for large procurements, as is done in Latvia, for instance.
- Systematic review:
  - SOE in Israel: annual review of engagements with third parties
  - SOE in Korea: ex post risk assessment in high-risk sectors such as large development projects covering more than a designated scale
  - Some SOEs in Norway: audits and unannounced inspections; nightly screening of all suppliers and customers
  - SOE inthe United Kingdom: Audit and Risk Committee Review all procurement where there has been a single tender process

Additional controls that companies consider useful for managing third parties include (i) establishment of policies on gifts, bribery, anti-money laundering and the like, discussed above, and (ii) confidential advice and whistleblowing channels, and effective internal audit, that are discussed below.

While participating companies exhibit a range of controls and procedures designed to manage risks of external engagement, there is room for strengthening company approaches in view of the challenges discussed in Chapter 1. Only 39% of companies require the integrity function (usually housed in internal audit or legal departments) to conduct due diligence for third parties.

Exceptions to an otherwise systematic approach to due diligence should be based on sound risk assessments for the project or engagement in question. Some practices and approaches are not systematically applied within companies, while others adopt ongoing monitoring of third and counterparties, regardless of the status and longevity of engagement. One European SOE conducts ex ante assessment of third parties only if the other company is unknown to the SOE. Another European company supplements memoranda for fair and open cooperation for only certain contracts.

The UNCAC calls for state parties to "consider corruption a relevant factor in legal proceedings to annul or rescind a contract, withdraw a concession or other similar instrument or take any other remedial action (34)" (UNCAC, 2003). SOEs too should be encouraged to consider such actions in face of corruption. Yet, SOEs appear less willing or able to sever business relations with partners than do private sector companies (Table 2.7). It could be hypothesised that SOEs are less exposed to potentially corrupt partners than private companies, but this is unlikely. The OECD's Foreign Bribery Report showed that the highest proportion and highest amount of foreign bribes were offered, promised or given to SOE officials over other public officials. Further, an IMF study showed that the majority of respondents' attributed corruption in the real sector to the SOE sector (IMF, 2017).

Table 2.7. Severing business relations in face of corruption risks: SOEs versus non-SOEs

Action	SOEs	Non-SOEs
Respondents that said their companies severed a relationship with at least one business partner (e.g. supplier, service provider) because of the risk of exposure to or engaging in corruption.	32%	66%

Note: The SOE data is based on 261 individual responses. The non-SOE data is based on 57 private sector respondents.
Source: OECD 2017 Survey of anti-corruption and integrity in SOEs; OECD (2016), Trust and Business.

Box 2.7. State-owned enterprises and public procurement: rules and regulations

As indicated in Chapter 1, public procurement and contract violations are amongst the top risks for SOEs. Accordingly, public procurement is treated explicitly in the SOE Guidelines: When SOEs engage in public procurement, whether as bidder or procurer, the procedures involved should be competitive, non-discriminatory and be safeguarded by appropriate standards of transparency (III. G.).

Countries concerned about the participation of SOEs in public procurement processes and in levelling the playing field have increasingly sought to ensure that regulations do not favour any category of bidder. Yet it differs by country whether or not these rules apply to SOEs in a similar manner to other government entities, as does the degree of implementation. Where SOEs fulfil a governmental purpose (have mixed objectives), or to the extent that a particular activity allows an SOE to fulfil such a purpose, the SOE should adopt government procurement guidelines that ensure a level playing field for all competitors (OECD, 2015).

- Eighty-six percent of respondents whose companies have specific rules for engaging in public procurement as a bidder (i.e. to act as the supplier of goods and services to other parts of the public sector) report to be subject to competitive bidding on an equal footing with other firms. However, respondents pointed most commonly to collusion and bid rigging as risks their companies face in engaging in public procurement.
- Similarly, 94% of respondents whose companies have specific rules for engaging in procurement as procurer (to procure goods and services) report being subject to government procurement rules. A few respondents reported being subject to additional rules specific to the SOE or to the sector of operation (e.g. energy).

Source: OECD 2017 Survey of anti-corruption and integrity in SOEs; OECD (2015b), OECD Guidelines on Corporate Governance of State-Owned Enterprises, 2015 Edition, OECD Publishing, Paris. http://dx.doi.org/10.1787/9789264244160-en.

As demonstrated by aforementioned company practices, third-party or counterparty management is applied commonly when companies engage in public procurement or other contracting. Box 2.7 details which laws are in place to support competitive neutrality and integrity and efficiency when SOEs engage in public procurement. SOEs may also derive use from the list of "integrity tools" for procurement, provided in Box 2.8. While the tools are directed at public sector entities responsible for the public procurement process, SOEs too could apply them to their own contracting processes.

Box 2.8 provides a checklist of public sector integrity tools applied to the public procurement cycle that can be employed in pursuit of the 2015 OECD Recommendation of the Council on Public Procurement.

Box 2.8. A checklist: public sector integrity tools tailored to public procurement

B.1 Adherents [to the 2015 OECD Recommendation of the Council on Public Procurement] should develop and implement risk assessment and management strategies and tools to safeguard integrity in the different stages of the procurement process. Those strategies and tools can include:

- needs assessments to ensure that the procurement project is needed in the first place (and not improperly influenced)
- risk maps to identify the positions, activities, and projects which are vulnerable, assessing probability and potential impact of risks of fraud and corruption
- red flags, standardised warning signs that stretch over the whole procurement cycle and assist in the detection of wrongdoing
- integrity plans (that facilitate the development of mitigation strategies)
- whistleblower programmes (that can mitigate risk-management pitfalls).

B.2 Adherents should develop and implement mechanisms to prevent for misconduct in public procurement. Those mechanisms could be the following:

- mechanisms that ensure the independent responsibility of at least two persons in the decision-making and control process -- the four-eye principle (double signatures, crosschecking, separation of duties and authorisation, etc.)
- systems of multiple-level review and approval of procurement process stages (reviews by independent senior officials independent of the procurement and project officials or by a specific contract review committee process)
- the rotation of officials, involving new responsibilities, as a safeguard for positions that involve long-term commercial connections for instance
- electronic systems for avoiding direct contact between officials and potential suppliers and for standardising processes
- adequate security control measures for handling of information (unique user identity codes, well-defined levels of computer access rights and procurement authority, encryption of confidential data)
- standardisation of bidding documents and procurement documentation,
- strong internal control and risk management mechanisms

- direct social controls on government activities through the introduction of social witnesses and social observers (who should ideally be trained in public procurement)
- other mechanisms such as the two-envelope approach and integrity monitors.

B.3 Adherents should develop and implement mechanisms for the detection and sanctioning of misconduct in public procurement. Those mechanisms could be the following:

- the systematic recording and tracking of key decisions (e.g. through electronic systems)
- red flags or other systems that provide warnings of irregularities and potential corruption
- exchange of information between officials in charge of control and investigation such as public procurers, internal controllers, auditors and competition authorities (e.g. specific joint training, expert assistance to gather evidence of corruption and collusion in public procurement, joint investigations, exchange of staff), and/or
- specific sanctions for misconduct in public procurement
- transparency of information to allow for "social control" of procurement activities.

Source: OECD (2016a), *Checklist for Supporting the Implementation of the OECD Recommendation of the Council on Public Procurement*, www.oecd.org/governance/procurement/toolbox/search/checklist-implementation-oecd-recommendation.pdf.

Element 6: Education and training on anti-corruption and integrity

Disseminating a culture of integrity is a cornerstone of an effective anti-corruption and integrity effort that encourages "doing the right thing". It helps the company to avoid waste on programmes and controls that are not understood and employed.

Companies in the survey allocate approximately 1.5% of operational budget to promoting integrity and mitigating corruption. Forty-five percent of respondents see this allocation of operational budget to fighting corruption and promoting integrity as an investment, with 25% seeing it as a cost, and the remainder with no or another view. Board members and those in charge of compliance, risk, legal or other saw it as more of an investment than did executive management, but not by a large margin. There is room for improvement in disseminating a tone from the top through executive management and through to all employees of the business benefits and growth and investment opportunities of a good reputation.

Fifty-seven percent of SOE respondents report that their companies provide training for all employees, board members and executive management, yet findings of Chapter 1 point to their ineffectiveness. SOE respondents pointed to both a lack of awareness and priority on integrity, and to perverse incentives that could detract SOE officials from "doing the right thing".

One of the greatest challenges to integrity in the participating companies was a lack of awareness of related requirements. Companies can increase the value-for-money of their investments in integrity by ensuring that trainings are effective in remedying some of the issues raised in this report. A PwC (2016) survey showed that while 82% of companies reported having an ethics and compliance programme in place, one in five respondents were not aware of it and many were confused about who owns it internally.

Box 2.9. Sample compliance assessment checklist: testing employee awareness, and effectiveness of training and communication

The *Anti-Corruption Ethics and Compliance Handbook for Business* explains how one UK-based international company uses self-assessment as one way to monitor compliance. When the self-assessment tool is applied testing employee awareness and effectiveness of training and communication, the unit head seeks to affirm the following:

My staff are aware of and understand the group AB&C policy, Code of Conduct and processes regarding gifts, hospitality and entertainment and have completed any required compliance training:

1. My staff are aware of the identity of their Local Compliance Officer, Divisional Compliance Officer (if different) and the Group Compliance Officer and when and how to contact them for advice or guidance.
2. My staff are aware of and understand [company]'s policy on facilitation payments and their duty to report such immediately to the Legal Department.
3. My staff are aware of and understand their duty to report promptly any concerns they may have whether relating to their own actions or the actions of others and how and when to use the group gifts and entertainment register and "whistleblowing" facility.
4. My staff are aware that there must be no retaliation against good faith "whistleblowers".

Source: OECD, United Nations Office on Drugs and Crime (UNODC) and the World Bank, Anti-Corruption Ethics and Compliance Handbook for Business (2013), www.oecd.org/corruption/anti-corruption-ethics-and-compliance-handbook-for-business.htm.

A focus on improving the effectiveness of education and training would be beneficial. The findings that such programmes are treated as a check-the-box exercises, without being taken seriously, present an opportunity to consider new approaches. Company examples could be used to draw inspiration on innovative ways to promote and cultivate a culture of integrity:

- A Korean SOE asks all employees including board members and senior management to take a vow of integrity.
- An Italian SOE invests in continuous training programmes in Italy and abroad that provide guidance on how to recognise and manage red flags.
- Another Italian company directly provides induction to top management and employees of the company, dedicated internal communications (e.g. newsletters and other), best practice sharing through dissemination of corporate governance tools and guidelines. They are committed to the achievement of compliance certifications (such as ISO 37001) .

- A German company does a "tone from the middle" survey every two years to assess perceptions at lower levels of the entity.
- An SOE in Costa Rica uses annual ethics tests of employees to assess their understanding of ethics requirements and to inform improvements in related mechanisms.

Box 2.9 provides a sample compliance assessment checklist to test employee awareness, and effectiveness of training and communication, as provided in the *Anti-Corruption Ethics and Compliance Handbook for Business* (2013), of the OECD, UNODC and World Bank.

Element 7: Disclosure, monitoring and auditing

The SOE Guidelines (2015b) require state-owned enterprises to "observe high standards of transparency and be subject to the same high quality accounting, disclosure, compliance and auditing standards as listed companies".

Disclosure

As a baseline, all SOEs should disclose material financial and non-financial information on the enterprise, including areas of significant concern for the state as an owner and the general public. Large and listed SOEs should disclose according to high quality internationally recognised standards.

An SOEs' disclosure should be dictated by a clear disclosure policy developed by the ownership entity. It should identify what information should be publicly disclosed, the appropriate channels for disclosure and the mechanisms for ensuring quality of information. The practice of embedding anti-corruption and integrity considerations into the state's disclosure policy is discussed in Chapter 3.

Table 2.8. Level of state-owned enterprise disclosure

Information to be disclosed	Percentage of respondents whose companies disclose each
1. A clear statement to the public of enterprise objectives and their fulfilment (for fully-owned SOEs this would include any mandate elaborated by the state ownership entity);	78%
2. Enterprise financial and operating results, including where relevant the costs and funding arrangements pertaining to public policy objectives;	96%
3. The governance, ownership and voting structure of the enterprise, including the content of any corporate governance code or policy and implementation processes;	81%
4. The remuneration of board members and key executives;	72%
5. Board member qualifications, selection process, including board diversity policies, roles on other company boards and whether they are considered as independent by the SOE board;	52%
6. Any material foreseeable risk factors and measures taken to manage such risks;	34%
7. Any financial assistance, including guarantees, received from the state and commitments made on behalf of the SOE, including contractual commitments and liabilities arising from public-private partnerships;	40%
8. Any material transactions with the state and other related entities;	43%

Note: The elements for disclosure are taken from the SOE Guidelines as examples of what could be disclosed, depending on the size and capacity of the SOE. Based on individual responses of 346 SOE respondents, from across 212 companies in 34 countries.
Source: OECD 2017 Survey of anti-corruption and integrity in SOEs.

Table 2.8 provides an overview of the degree to which participating SOEs disclose recommended financial and non-financial information. Thirty-four percent of SOEs disclose material foreseeable risk factors and measures taken to manage such risks, recalling that one in ten companies do not explicitly treat corruption risks as part of risk assessments. Red flags may be falling between the cracks.

Almost half of participating SOEs report on their anti-corruption and integrity efforts and policies in the annual report (44%). Fifteen percent of respondents' companies only report through internal documents and one percent does not report at all (Figure 2.4).

Figure 2.4. Channels for reporting on company integrity policies or anti-corruption efforts

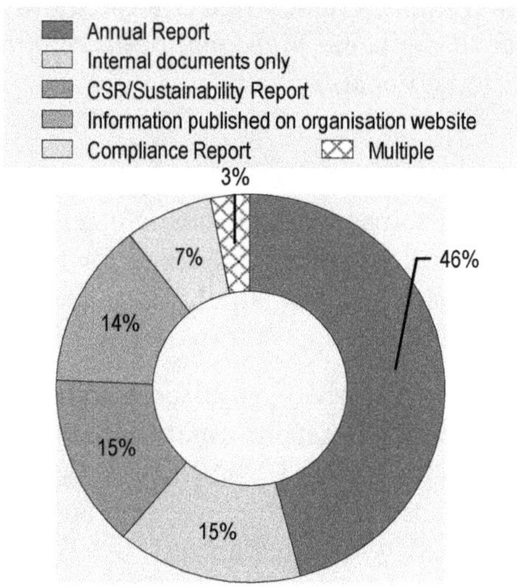

Note: Based on 347 individual responses about their company, to "How, if at all, is information reported on your company's integrity policies or anti-corruption efforts?"
Source: OECD 2017 Survey of anti-corruption and integrity in SOEs.

Internal audit

Internal audit is an independent and objective assurance activity evaluating the effectiveness of a company's risk management, control and governance. It is important to the achievement of a company's objectives and supportive of integrity in the company. Moreover, internal audit can further support anti-corruption and integrity efforts in a company by making it a specific audit topic – for instance, assessing the effectiveness of specific controls related to bribery, or, for instance, the effectiveness of an anti-corruption programme's implementation.

Ninety-two percent of participating SOEs report having an internal audit function, and 84% assign it as at least one of the units or departments with significant responsibility for integrity. Yet, 25% found its ineffectiveness poses obstacles to their company's integrity. This sub-section considers why.

Sixty four percent of SOEs in the sample are required by law to establish internal audit - the majority of which were required to do so in line with other government departments or agencies. Eighteen percent of all companies are aligned with listed company requirements and 7% with privately incorporated companies (Figure 2.5). One quarter of the sample report that internal audit was established voluntarily, not mandatorily. Finally, 4% (eight companies of an eligible 180) do not have internal audit.

Figure 2.5. Requirements for internal audit in state-owned enterprises

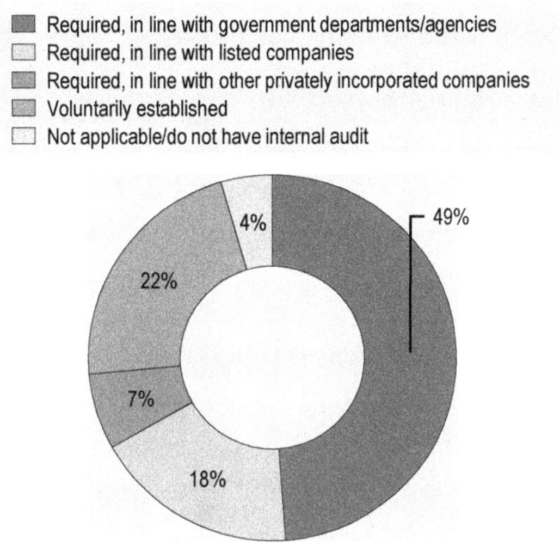

Note: Based on aggregated and comparable responses of 180 SOEs to the question "please best describe your company's internal audit unit/function".
Source: OECD 2017 Survey of anti-corruption and integrity in SOEs.

Figure 2.6 compares the incidence of corruption within companies with the more commonly applied internal audit functions. The findings show that respondents in companies that have internal audit requirements in line with listed companies were more likely to see corruption (57%), compared to those in line with government departments or agencies (40%) and those which voluntarily established internal audit without a requirement (25%). It may be recalled that 42% of respondents report to have witnessed corruption or other irregular practices materialise in the last three years in their company.

Figure 2.6. Witnesses to corruption in companies with different internal audit requirements

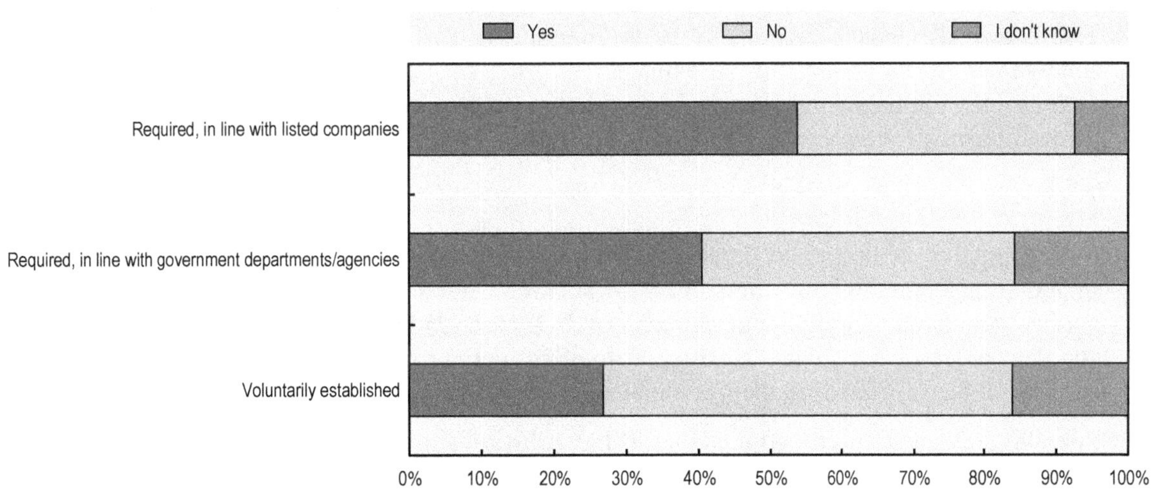

Note: Based on 230 individual responses that fell into the three categories of each question: "Please best describe your company's internal audit unit/function" and "in your assessment, did any of the [listed] risks materialise into activities/actions in the last three years in (or involving) your company?"
Source: OECD 2017 Survey of anti-corruption and integrity in SOEs.

The 25% of SOE respondents rated "ineffective internal audit" as at least "somewhat of an obstacle to integrity" in their company were more likely to be:

- board members or executive management, as opposed to those in charge of compliance, internal audit, or risk;
- in companies where internal audit is "required in line with government departments/agencies";
- in companies operating with SOE-specific law and with mixed objectives (commercial with public policy).

Of those who rated "ineffective internal audit" as at least "somewhat of an obstacle to integrity", 44% had witnessed corrupt or other irregular practices in their company in the last three years – slightly higher than the average of all respondents (42%).

On average, companies' internal audit departments undertake two of the three following audits: financial, compliance and performance (or operational). Most often, companies conduct compliance audits (88% of respondents' companies), financial audits (82%) followed by performance audits (71%). Performance audits are usually targeted at efficiency, effectiveness and economy of company processes, and may include, for instance, assessments of quality management systems and of information protection and security. IT audits are also common.

A survey on internal auditors' perceptions – the Institute of Internal Auditors' Global Internal Audit Common Body of Knowledge Stakeholder Survey (2015) – suggests that the more tools they have at their disposal for the execution of their duties, the more value added. While it is good practice for SOEs' annual financial statements to be subject to an independent external audit based on high-quality standards (OECD, 2015b: VI.B), SOEs may also wish to systematise performance auditing that looks at the efficiency and effectiveness of integrity mechanisms in the context of broader corporate governance.

Internal audit, and any audit committee, plays an important oversight role in achievement of objectives. Yet internal audit is not synonymous with monitoring or investing in corruption detection. Internal audit units or departments should not be used as a crutch or replacement for the role of the board in monitoring overall performance of the company. The board also has a responsibility in monitoring the performance of the SOE, the achievement of its goals, and the management of risks – corruption and other – that may detract from such achievement. The board however, may rely on internal audits to inform its monitoring process.

External audit

In conjunction with the SOE Guidelines' recommendation for internal audit, SOEs' financial statements should be subject to an independent external audit based on high-quality standards. Twenty-four percent of SOE respondents saw "ineffective external audit" as at least "somewhat an obstacle" to effectively promoting integrity and preventing corruption in, or involving, their companies.

Specific state control procedures should not substitute for an independent external audit (OECD, 2015b). In many countries, the SAI provides oversight, insight and foresight on governance within and across SOEs, as well as of the governance arrangements between SOEs and the state ownership entity. The SAI should not attempt to duplicate such financial audits but should rather focus the audits on the performance and efficiency of SOEs, directing recommendations to the state ownership entity. Examples include:

- a grading of management control environments and financial systems and controls for SOEs, by New Zealand's Office of the Auditor General
- the National Audit Office of the UK's value-for-money audit on the existence and structure of SOEs
- audit of the sustainability of SOEs by Portugal's Tribunal de Contas.

In many countries, notably in Latin America, SOEs are not fully corporatised, or are operated in close proximity to the public administration and are thus often subject to more direct state financial control. The relationship between state auditors and SOEs depends in large part on the institutional arrangements for state ownership and the degree of corporatisation of the SOE sector.

Some SAIs may have a broader role than in performance audits of individual or a group of SOEs. In Italy some cases[8] defined by Law No. 259/1958, a representative from Italy's SAI - the "Corte dei Conti" - will take part in the meetings of the board of statutory auditors on the board of directors. In Chile, the Contraloria Generale de la Republica undertakes ex ante approval of particular contracts over the threshold amount for the public administration.

Effective monitoring by the board

The board is responsible for monitoring management. Performance monitoring should integrate board expectations for responsible business conduct – an important component of which is anti-corruption and integrity (OECD, 2015b: VI). Section 2.2.3 showed that boards are more informed than executive management on most audit findings and integrity-related assessments.

Boards must be well informed in order to adequately monitor the performance of management, including with respect to integrity and anti-corruption. Boards, to a certain degree rely on the determination of management as to what is materially significant and thus should be shared with the board.

The presence of specific audit, risk or compliance committees may facilitate more regular discussion on the topics. The presence of specialised board committees is associated with fewer reported instances of corrupt or other irregular practices in a company.

The findings in this report may also motivate the board to integrate anti-corruption and integrity performance into board assessments of management. With regards to anti-corruption mechanisms or programmes, boards should have appropriate assurance of the performance of integrity mechanisms and related controls. In 86% of companies, the department assigned significant responsibility for integrity is also responsible for overseeing implementation of internal guidelines or codes.

Key findings that may be useful for monitoring are not always shared with boards (see Table 2.9). A broader range of integrity related outputs are shared with them than with executive management, except in two areas: recommendations from integrity functions and evaluations of internal controls (that may be separate from internal audits). It is possible that boards are missing the complete picture. Indeed, the findings in Chapter 1 demonstrated that board members and executive management have different perspectives on corruption risk in the company, and that these are not aligned with the real incidence of corruption.

Table 2.9. Which assessments and audit findings are presented to state-owned enterprise leadership?

List of recommendations/ findings	% of respondents whose companies present such findings to the:	
	Board	Executive Management
Findings of risk assessments that point to integrity or corruption risks	**71**	66
Internal audit findings/recommendations	**83**	71
External audit findings/recommendations	**83**	66
Recommendations from integrity functions	49	**58**
Evaluations of internal controls (that may be separate from internal audits)	32	**36**
Reports or claims of irregular practices or corruption made through reporting channels	**59**	57

Source: OECD 2017 Survey of anti-corruption and integrity in SOEs.

There is scope for integrating anti-corruption efforts into company targets and performance appraisal, with associated indicators for measurement. For instance, one Korean SOE has linked integrity into its long-term strategies and goals. The company is meant to (i) constitute the "highest degree" integrity culture, (ii) strengthen control and prevention of corruption, and (iii) establish human rights management. The company has established associated indicators that are internally and externally verified to track their success:

- the external assessment includes evaluations of: (a) integrity, (b) corruption-prevention policies, and (c) of the Korea Business Ethic Index: Sustainable management (KoBEX-SM)
- the internal assessment includes evaluations of (a) integrity, (b) risk assessment of executive members, and (c) the ethical management index, and a "red-face test".

Box 2.10 highlights suggested elements of a checklist, prepared by Transparency International UK (2012), for monitoring and evaluation of anti-bribery programmes, that may be applicable and informative for other integrity-related mechanisms and programmes that go beyond the scope of bribery.

Box 2.10. Transparency International UK's checklist: Monitoring and review of anti-bribery programmes

- Continuing and/or discrete evaluations are performed supporting the continuous improvement of the programme.
- The company use key performance indicators to encourage and measure progress in improvement of the programme and its implementation. Discussions are held with stakeholders especially suppliers and contractors to obtain their views on the programme
- The company benchmarks its programme internally between business units The company benchmarks its programme externally
- There is a procedure for ensuring that there is an adequate audit trail to support all recorded transactions.

- There is a procedure to discuss the results of internal audits of the Programme with relevant operational personnel.
- There is a procedure to address weaknesses identified through internal audits with a documented corrective action plan and a timetable for action.
- External consultants are used to monitor and advise on the programme.
- The company participates in anti-corruption initiatives and business sector groups to learn best practices to improve its programme.
- Self-evaluations are carried out and the results applied to improve the programme.
- There is a procedure to ensure that the internal control systems, in particular the accounting and record keeping practices, are subject to regular internal audits to provide assurance that they are effective in countering bribery.
- There is a procedure for senior management to monitor the programme and periodically review its suitability, adequacy and effectiveness and implement improvements as appropriate.
- There is there a procedure for senior management to periodically report the results of programme reviews to the audit committee, governance committee, board or equivalent body.
- There is a procedure for prompt reporting of any issues or concerns to senior management and the board.
- There is a procedure for the audit committee, governance committee, the board or equivalent body to make an independent assessment of the adequacy of the Programme.
- There is a procedure for the audit committee, to report regularly to the board on its independent assessment of the adequacy of the programme.
- There is a procedure to use the experience from incidents to improve the programme.
- The company has a procedure for self-reporting bribery incidents as appropriate to the authorities.
- The board or equivalent body has considered whether to commission external verification or assurance of the programme.
- An external verification or assurance has been conducted.
- The verification or assurance opinion has been published publicly.
- The company publishes publicly a description of the scope and frequency of feedback mechanisms and other internal processes supporting the continuous improvement of the programme.
- The company publishes publicly a description of the company's procedure for investigation and resolution of incidents.
- The company publishes publicly details of public legal cases of bribery involving the company.

Source: Wilkinson, Peter, and Transparency International UK (2012), The 2010 UK Bribery Act, Adequate Procedures Checklist, Guidance on good practice procedures for corporate anti-bribery programmes, Transparency International UK, 2010, London, www.transparency.org.uk/wp-content/plugins/download-attachments/includes/download.php?id=986.

Element 8: Detection, advice and complaint channels

Detection

Detection makes use of the mechanisms discussed above, including internal audit, external audit, internal controls and complaints channels. International studies on corruption and fraud, corporate misconduct or other irregular practices in the public and private sectors, consistently show internal audit and reporting channels as the most effective means of detection (Table 2.10). This holds for detection of general irregular practices as well as with specific forms of it including foreign bribery and fraud.

Table 2.10. What are the most effective detection and assurance mechanisms?

Category	General	Specific to foreign bribery	Specific to fraud	Effectiveness of business ethics and compliance programmes
Report	Control Risks' *International Business Attitudes to Compliance* (2017)	OECD's *Detection of Foreign Bribery* (2017)	The Association of Certified Fraud Examiners' 2017 *Global Fraud Survey*	PwC's *Global Economic Crime Survey* (2016)
Findings	Anonymous whistleblower line or reporting mechanism (64%), A known person or team within the organisation responsible for responding (59%), Anti-corruption compliance audits (41%), Data analytics to monitor transactions in real time (34%), Post-acquisition assessments (20%) Surprise fraud audits (18%) (Control Risks, 2017)	22% of foreign bribery cases were brought to the attention of law enforcement authorities through companies' self-reporting. These self-reporting entities became aware of foreign bribery in their business operations predominantly through internal audit (22%), internal controls/investigations (7%), mergers and acquisitions due diligence (7%) and whistleblowing (5%).	Tips (predominantly through telephone but also through email and through online or web-based forms) (39.1%), Internal audit (16.5%) Management review (13.4%)	76% internal audit, 54% management reporting, 42% monitoring whistleblowing hotline reports, 40% external audit, 6% other internal monitoring, 2% other external monitoring, 4% other

Note: The table does not allow for comparisons between studies, as they use different methodologies, but is instructive in demonstrating how internal audit features across studies.

Source: ACFE (2017), Report to the Nations on Occupational Fraud and Abuse, Global Fraud Survey, www.acfe.com/rttn2016/docs/2016-report-to-the-nations.pdf; Control Risks (2017), International Business Attitudes to Compliance, Report 2017, https://www.controlrisks.com/our-thinking/insights/reports/international-business-attitudes-to-compliance; OECD (2017b), The Detection of Foreign Bribery, www.oecd.org/corruption/the-detection-of-foreign-bribery.htm; OECD (2014), Foreign Bribery Report, http://dx.doi.org/10.1787/9789264226616-en; PwC (2016), Adjusting the Lens on Economic Crime, Global Economic Crime Survey, www.pwc.com/gx/en/economic-crime-survey/pdf/GlobalEconomicCrimeSurvey2016.pdf

Respondents that reported ineffective detection mechanisms (internal audit, whistleblowing, controls and external audit) reported in greater numbers to have witnessed corruption in their company in the last three years. Interestingly, their perception of the effectiveness of detection mechanisms did not change the overall perception of risk likelihood. This confirms that companies with weak detection do not rate present risks in line with perceptions that risks actually occurred in the past.

Forty-three percent of SOE respondents feel that their company's integrity is at least somewhat challenged by the general perception that the likelihood of being caught for misconduct is low. These companies, in which there is a perception that the likelihood of being caught is low, were more likely to report seeing corruption.

Confidential complaint and advice channels

In pursuit of the SOE Guidelines, ownership entities should ensure that SOEs are responsible for effectively establishing safe-harbours for complaints for employees, either personally or through their representative bodies, or for others outside the SOE. SOE boards could grant employees or their representatives a confidential direct access to someone independent on the board, or to an ombudsman within the enterprise (OECD, 2015b: V.C).

Such channels should be in place for those who wish to report violations of integrity policies or of corruption and other irregular practices, as well as for those who wish to not commit violations and who seek advice. This could include of those who are under pressure to violate rules from superiors (World Bank Group, 2010). Advice and complaint channels should provide a systematic mechanism to assess effectiveness of integrity mechanisms and to manage red flags in particular projects, or business areas.

The following reporting practices emerge from the companies of the 347 respondents:

- Most complaints channels are formalised as a whistleblower mechanism, with 60% of respondents reporting this to be the case. Almost half have online internal and external sites, and just less than half have another in-person option for lodging complaints to report suspected instances of corruption or irregular practices involving the company.
- On average, claims channels are usually open to, or claims are sent to, two individuals or positions within a company: most commonly to those in charge of legal, compliance, risk or audit. Thirty-eight respondent companies channel the information to the CEO or President, and 33% to a member of the board. Companies report that employees and officials are offered the choice of who to go to and how.
- Participating SOEs estimated that almost half, 48%, of all claims made through such channels in the last 12 months pertained to corruption or other related irregular practices.
- Some companies send such reports to specific units -- such as a high level whistleblowing committee; an ethics committee that is separate from the board as in one Italian company; a working group consisting of heads of HR, quality, security and of the management board as does one company in Latvia; an Ethics and Conflict of Interest Prevention Committee and Internal Oversight Department; or to a Chief Governance Officer in a Corporate Governance Office such as in the Philippines; or the quality department, the Ombudsman office, or an Investigation Department as is done in one company in Turkey.
- SOEs in the survey predominantly classify claims as confidential (60%). One third classifies them as anonymous, and the remainder are attributed to the individual making the claim or report (Figure 2.7).

Figure 2.7. Classification of claims: confidential, anonymous or attributed.

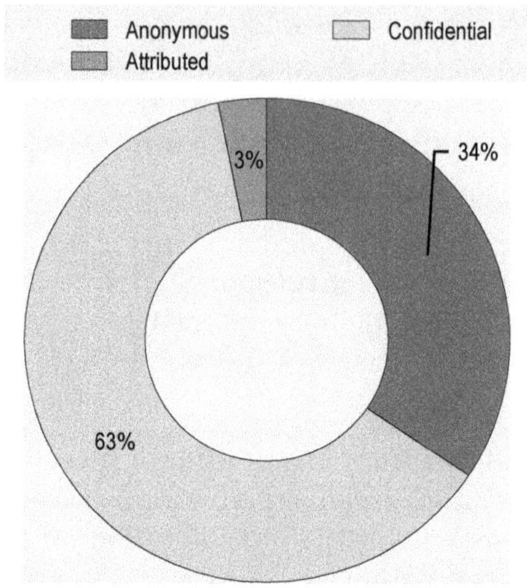

Note: Based on the 128 companies that knew how claims were categorised, or that could agree upon the classification (in companies with multiple respondents) in response to: "How are internal and external reports/claims about corruption or other irregular practices categorised/classified when coming through your company's reporting mechanism"?
Source: OECD 2017 Survey of anti-corruption and integrity in SOEs.

Three quarters of SOEs offer legal protection from discriminatory or disciplinary action for those who disclose wrongdoing in good faith on reasonable grounds, yet 21% do not. Those that do so are either required by law (45%) or have done so voluntarily (30%).

Of the 42% of respondents that have seen corruption or other irregular practices in their company in the last three years, 92% said they had reported it. One chief compliance officer from a European SOE admitted that he did not report what he saw as the anti-corruption programme had not yet been in place. Of the vast majority of respondents that reported witnessing corrupt or irregular activity, only two reported experiencing retaliation for doing so, which is a much lower rate than those found in another comparable international study (ECI, 2016).

Thirty-seven percent of SOE board members and executive management report that ineffectiveness of reporting channels and whistleblowing mechanisms as an obstacle to integrity in their company. This ranks it amongst the top ten obstacles to integrity of the participating SOEs. Companies should focus not only on the channels but the action undertaken by the reports. As mentioned above, SOEs appear less likely to take strict action (cancelling projects and taking remedial action, for instance) compared to other private companies.

A common concern is that those witnessing corruption will not report for fear of retaliation or discrimination, but only two who saw and reported corruption or other irregular practices experienced retaliation as a result. For one respondent, retaliation came in the form of increased time delays, administrative costs and friction in relationships. Retaliation for "doing the right thing" was generally ranked as a low likelihood of occurrence on average across participating countries.

The general finding that the vast majority were not retaliated against may signal that mechanisms for protecting whistleblowers are effective. Figure 2.8 shows that 70% of respondents report that their company has legal protection for those who disclose wrongdoing, 45% of which do so as required by law. An OECD survey on business integrity and corporate governance showed that over one third of companies surveyed did not have a written policy for protecting whistleblowers from reprisal (OECD, 2015a). OECD's *Committing to Effective Whistleblower Protection*, showed that while much progress has been made in whistleblower protection in the public sector that the private sector lagged behind (OECD, 2016b).

Figure 2.8. Protection for those disclosing or reporting wrong-doing in good faith

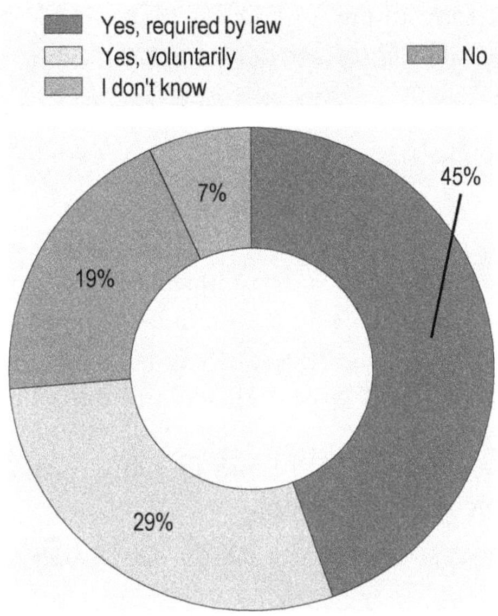

Note: Based on 129 companies that responded to the question and could agree (where multiple respondents) on the answer to the question "Does your company have legal protection from discriminatory or disciplinary action for those who disclose wrongdoing in good faith, to competent authorities, on reasonable grounds?"
Source: OECD 2017 Survey of anti-corruption and integrity in SOEs.

Another study by the Ethics and Compliance Initiative (2016) showed that of the 34% of respondents in the public sector had observed misconduct, and 32% in the private sector; The majority report the misconduct (59%, both categories), but at least one third (36%) experience retaliation for reporting (private sector 33% and public 41%).

Table 2.11. Mechanisms for ensuring legal protection for those who disclose wrongdoing in good faith

Ways to ensure legal protection	Reported company examples for legal protection of those reporting
Reliance on robustness of mechanisms for reporting/whistleblowing	Person reporting remains anonymous/confidential, training for all officials, encouraging a culture of reporting, "Whistleblower protection system"
Explicit references in company Codes or whistleblowing codes	Reference in national legislation, internal regulation, Code of Conduct/ethics, Policy for Workplace Harassment, Compliance Investigation Manual, etc.
Punitive measures for those retaliating or discriminating	Grounds for discipline (including retaliation),

Note: Based on the question "Does your company have legal protection from discriminatory or disciplinary action for those who disclose wrongdoing in good faith, to competent authorities, on reasonable grounds?" The Table is not meant to be comprehensive but to provide examples of different company approaches.
Source: OECD 2017 Survey of anti-corruption and integrity in SOEs.

Table 2.11 outlines the ways in which companies do ensure such legal protection in practice. One company provides protection from retaliation on a more subjective basis: if the person reporting is well intentioned and their claims are true. A few report that while protection through law exists that it is only partially guaranteed or it has not been applied. One company "guarantees discretion and confidentiality during the entire disclosure management process, from the time the disclosure is received to the preliminary investigation and conclusion phase".

Box 2.11 provides example questions that companies may use to self-assess the systems in place for reporting, as put forth in the OECD, UNODC and World Bank, *Anti-Corruption Ethics and Compliance Handbook for Business* (2013).

Box 2.11. Key questions to assess companies' systems for reporting and investigation

- Has management established a culture in which questions will be raised?
- Does management regularly communicate the requirement for reporting concerns?
- Does the business unit have a clearly defined plan for response to such concerns?
- Are procedures in place to ensure that any issues are communicated to the appropriate group function?

Source: OECD, UNODC and the World Bank, *Anti-Corruption Ethics and Compliance Handbook for Business* (2013), www.oecd.org/corruption/anti-corruption-ethics-and-compliance-handbook-for-business.htm.

Element 9: Incentives for integrity

OECD's Good Practice Guidance on Internal Controls, Ethics and Compliance asks companies to consider "appropriate measures to encourage and provide positive support for the observance of ethics and compliance programmes or measures against all foreign bribery [and corruption], at all levels of the company" (OECD, 2010). Company officials should be reassured that they will not suffer retaliation from refusing to engage in, or reporting on, corruption and other irregular practices, as discussed above in the section on detection and advice channels.

SOEs, and state ownership entities, should communicate the benefits of integrity and hindrance of corruption, raising awareness to the threat, causes and gravity of corruption. This approach is promoted by the UNCAC (2003). Positive reinforcement and awareness-raising is covered further in the section above on education and training.

SOEs should also seek to manage perverse incentives for corrupt behaviour that puts personal interest of themselves or another ahead of the best interest of the company and, importantly for the case of SOEs, ahead of society as an ultimate shareholder.

Incentives management should be incorporated into the risk management system. This means identifying and managing perverse incentives to misbehave, rule-break, or engage in corruption that may be exacerbated by an SOEs' governance structure, goals or objectives.

OECD's *Behavioural Insights for Public Integrity – Harnessing the Human Factor to Counter Corruption* (2018) provides insight into what public administrations, as well as SOEs and private sectors alike, can do about perverse incentives that may give rise to corruption. Table 2.12 outlines the Australian Government's "Values Alignment" framework to describe three types of persons based on their likelihood to engage in corruption and what can be done about it (ACLEI, 2017; OECD, 2017b; OECD, 2018). OECD's forthcoming work on behavioural insights for public sector integrity emphasise the potential in tapping into and focusing efforts on group B of Table 2.12 – where a culture of company integrity and awareness and education can help to negate existing perverse incentives.

Table 2.12. When values are aligned, or misaligned with the company's, and what can be done about it

Classification	Characteristics	What can be done?
Group A	Represents people who are unlikely to act corruptly regardless of circumstances, perhaps as a result of internal values or identity	Recruit for values that resist corruption
Group B	Represents people whose decision to act corruptly is dependent on circumstance. In ideal conditions, this group is unlikely to act corruptly. However, the opposite is true if personal or environmental circumstances were conducive	Provide a work environment for staff in which high professional standards are valued, opportunities for corrupt conduct are minimised and compliance with integrity measures is made easy
Group C	Represents a small group of people who are likely to act corruptly whenever they can get away with it. This group is driven by self-interest and tend to respond only to effective deterrence	Be prepared for the existence of the purely self-interested, by putting in place effective detection and deterrence measures

Source: Australian Commission for Law Enforcement Integrity, www.aclei.gov.au/corruption-prevention/key-concepts/values-alignment; OECD (2017c), *OECD Integrity Review of Colombia: Investing in Integrity for Peace and Prosperity*, OECD Publishing, Paris, http://dx.doi.org/10.1787/9789264278325-en; OECD (2018): *Behavioural Insights for Public Integrity – Harnessing the Human Factor to Counter Corruption.* OECD Public Governance Reviews, OECD Publishing, Paris, http://dx.doi.org/10.1787/9789264297067-en.

The 347 survey respondents (SOE board members and senior management) confirmed that behavioural considerations can challenge the efficacy of SOEs' corruption prevention. The following challenges were rated as "somewhat an obstacle", "an obstacle"; or "very much an obstacle" to effectively promoting integrity and preventing corruption in, or involving, their company:

- opportunistic behaviour of individuals (51%)
- a perception that the likelihood of getting caught is low (43%)
- a perception that the cost of corruption is low and/or return is high (38%).

Respondents that see these behavioural issues as obstacles to SOE integrity have also seen more corruption and other irregular practices in the last three years, and rate the likelihood and impact of future risks transpiring as higher.

Liability regimes may affect the behaviour of SOE representatives with respect to corruption and other irregular practices. The above factors are considered greater obstacles in SOEs that operate under a criminal liability regime in which the entity is liable only when senior management (in the "directing mind" and will of the company) committed the crime (sometimes known as the identification doctrine or theory) (OECD, 2016c). In these companies, those in "the directing mind" of the company may put pressure on lower ranks to break rules. Indeed, non-management employees and mid-level managers are considered by respondents to be most often involved in corruption. On the contrary, SOEs operating under "strict" or "adjusted" liability regimes, where the entire company is liable for criminal wrong-doing, see the above factors as less of an obstacle to their company's effective prevention and detection of corruption.

The "fraud triangle" described in PwC (2011) outlines three common factors that are in place when fraud occurs that may be applicable to corrupt or irregular practices:

- **Opportunistic behaviour**: PwC's 2016 Global Economic Crime Survey found that economic crime was primarily a result of the opportunity or ability to commit the crime (69%), compared to incentives or pressure to perform (14%) (PwC, 2016a).
- **Pressure or incentive to engage in misconduct**: A report by the Financial Stability Board (FSB, 2017), identifies the root causes of misconduct in the financial sector. Findings show that misconduct follows a trail that begins with some form of pressure, thereby affecting decisions by leadership or tone from the top and ultimately contributing to an organisational culture that undervalues safety and ethical values. The report also finds that a lack of appropriate governance arrangements may provide incentives to engage in misconduct, including but not limited to unclear roles and responsibilities and insufficient controls.
- **Justification or rationalisation of the behaviour**: A global survey by Ernst and Young (EY, 2016) finds that executive management, notably chief financial officers, can justify misconduct when under financial pressure. The PwC Global Economic Crime survey found that 11% of perpetrators of economic crime used rationalisations to justify their behaviour (PwC, 2016a).

These three common denominators of fraud are applied in this report to corrupt and other irregular practices in SOEs. A blatant form of pressure is the direct pressure to break rules, or to compromise integrity standards. One study (ECI, 2016) found that pressure to compromise standards was higher in:

- **multinationals** (25%) as opposed to solely domestic companies (18%)[9]
- **companies that are suppliers** have more pressure to compromise standards than those that are not (26% versus 18%)[10]
- companies undergoing **numerous and recent organisational changes**.

SOEs should monitor red flags for individuals' behaviour as part of the overall risk management system of the enterprise. A study conducted biennially by the ACFE has, since 2008, consistently found six top red flags that may help to identify those who commit occupational fraud: (i) living beyond their means, (ii) financial difficulties, (iii) unusually close association with vendors or customers, (iv) "wheeler-dealer" attitudes, (v) control issues or unwillingness to share duties, and (vi) personal or family issues. In almost 80% of the cases of occupational fraud that were studied, perpetrators exhibited at least one of these six flags. While the findings focus on occupational fraud, the study also found that 37.4% of all cases were an overlap of fraud and corruption and/or asset mismanagement (ACFE, 2016).

It should be clear to corporate insiders that engagement in corrupt or other irregular practices has implications that extend beyond the financial. SOEs in this study have indeed suffered financial losses to corruption or other irregular practices. In 47% of companies, at least one representative reported that the company lost operational budget due to corruption and other irregular practices. They estimate the losses to be at 1.4% of annual corporate profits. In some cases, this figure included cost estimates relating to compliance with enforcement actions or sanctions that have been paid.

Box 2.12. Countering perverse incentives: A maturity framework for developing a positive culture

Fundamental

- Officials understand and agree the need and value of effective risk management.
- Senior executives and line managers demonstrate the importance the entity places on managing risk in line with the entity's framework and systems.

Developed

- The entity's risk management framework is integral to its operating model.
- Lessons learnt are communicated to staff.
- There is a common understanding of the meaning of good risk management and as a result a consistent use of language and understanding of risk related concepts.

Systematic

- Surveys and external reviews undertaken (such as the annual state of the service report or capability reviews) are analysed to provide insights into the risk culture of the entity.
- The entity analyses loss incidents and identifies areas for improvement. This includes acknowledging good risk management practice and speaking with staff regularly about opportunities to better manage risk.

Integrated

- Senior executives are held accountable through their performance agreements for managing risk including responsibility for strengthening the risk culture of their teams.
- The entity's risk culture is formally and regularly assessed with recommendations identified for improvement.
- The entity has a risk management framework that is integrated with its overarching governance framework so that the task of managing risk is not regarded as an additional responsibility or burden.

Advanced

- Officials are comfortable raising concerns with senior managers and those being challenged respond positively.
- There is a sponsor at the senior executive level of the entity that leads and promotes the management of risk across the entity.
- The entity learns from negative and positive situations so that policy and procedural changes are made to improve the management of risk in the future.

Optimal

- The culture of the entity is one that demonstrates and promotes an open and proactive approach to managing risk that considers both threat and opportunity.
- Examples of good risk management practice are communicated by senior executives and individuals that excel in demonstrating good risk management practice in their day to day responsibilities are rewarded.

Source: Government of Australia, Department of Finance (2017), *Benchmarking Survey 2017 – Risk Management Maturity Capability Levels* (2017), www.finance.gov.au/sites/default/files/rm-capability-maturity-levels-2017.pdf.

The greatest casualty of economic crime is employee morale, according to another international study (PwC, 2016a). SOEs should pay attention to low employee morale and the working environment this creates because, as mentioned above, individual actions may be dependent on the conduciveness of an environment to promoting positive incentives for integrity. Employee morale as a casualty of corruption may only serve to deepen the issue.

SOEs do not operate in a vacuum. SOEs in this study are also concerned with reputational damage, and subsequent loss of trust and client base. SOEs should give due consideration and care to the economic, social and environmental externalities of their actions, not least to their involvement in corrupt or other irregular practices.

Box 2.12 elaborates a maturity model for developing a positive culture within an entity. While applied to improving the culture of risk management in an entity, it can be used as inspiration and tailored to improving a culture of integrity more broadly in response to the above behavioural risks. The "optimal" practice includes a situation where "examples of good risk management practice are communicated by senior executives and individuals that excel in demonstrating good risk management practice in their day to day responsibilities are rewarded" (Australian Government Department of Finance, 2017). It can be useful, in particular, for targeting "Group B" in Table 2.11, for whom a positive environment can effectively persuade people to "do the right thing".

Element 10: Investigation, response and improvement: what happens when things go wrong?

In case of suspected wrong-doing, SOEs would benefit from having techniques to manage efficiently, effectively and economically. International good practice suggests that companies have in place (i) appropriate disciplinary measures and procedures to address corruption and other irregular practices (OECD's Good Practice Guidance); (ii) the ability to apply appropriate sanctions for violations of integrity mechanisms or programmes internally (Principles for Countering Bribery); (iii) investigative procedures (Integrity Compliance Guidelines); (iv) openness to cooperate appropriately with relevant authorities in connection with investigations and prosecutions (Business Principles for Countering Bribery).

SOEs in this study usually assign internal audit units, legal departments and HR departments with primary responsibility for internal investigations and for remedial or disciplinary action for violation of integrity policies. These units are additionally responsible for overseeing implementation of internal guidelines or codes in 65% of respondents companies.

Where red flags are detected, or in cases of suspected corruption or other irregular practices, SOEs generally take a first step of launching an internal investigation before, if needed, appealing to external authorities for further investigation.

In a case in Colombia, it was the board of directors that noticed a series of inconsistencies in its financial and operational results of the company and later decided to conduct an in-depth restructuring process and commanded a forensic external audit, which later confirmed their concerns. In the Netherlands, an external investigation was requested by the board and the Ministry of Finance in its capacity as shareholder, to carry out a thorough analysis of the effectiveness of the existing internal procedures, risk management, compliance and checks within an SOE involved in corruption, and all its subsidiaries. The SOE took on additional measures based on the external report to refine internal procedures and checks and it has drawn up an action plan preventing bribery and corruption in the future. Upon suspicion of one case of corruption in Argentina, the national internal audit agency in Argentina (SIGEN) was the one to raise the case with authorities and communicated the facts to the Anti-Corruption Agency, which took the case to the Courts.

Suspected and real corruption and other irregular practices should be accompanied or followed by an internal review and, if necessary, revision of existing integrity mechanisms – including a root-cause analysis of what went wrong. It may also warrant an external review. Such activities should complement the aforementioned, regular and robust monitoring of the integrity mechanisms or programme by the designated party, as well as overall performance monitoring of management by the board.

Impact, response and improvement

Penalties and their severity for corruption or other irregular practices will vary, and may include the following, based on real cases presented by SOEs and state ownership entities participating in this study:

- civil or criminal fines or sanctions
- imprisonment
- debarment
- dissolution
- organisational restructuring and/or removal of officials or board members
- increased monitoring
- requirements to improve or overhaul integrity measures and/or to or implement compliance or anti-corruption programmes.

Following a corruption investigation in a Dutch SOE, the board chairman, under whose responsibility irregularities took place, left the company. There were additional criminal procedures against some former directors. The SOE's board of directors was expanded to include a portfolio of Governance, Risk and Compliance. Internal procedures and codes of conduct for procurement (and compliance with them) have been tightened.

In one corruption case, individuals in a Colombian SOE were handed seven prison sentences. Executives in the third-party company with whom the bribery occurred received fines, and the third-party company was debarred and subject to increased monitoring through the SOEs' compliance division.

The OECD's Foreign Bribery Report (2014) found that the majority of the 427 foreign bribery cases concluded between 1999 and 2014 resulted predominantly in civil or criminal fines (261). Other types of punishment included confiscation (82), imprisonment (80), compliance programmes (70), injunction (67), suspended prison sentence (38), compensation (12), debarment (2) and dissolution (1). Of the cases for which data was available, 46% had a sanction that was less than 50% of the proceeds obtained by the defendant as a result of bribery foreign public officials. In 13% of cases, the sanction was 50-100% of the profits, in 19% of cases it was 100-200% and in 22% cases it was greater than 200% of the proceeds of the bribe.

SOEs have suffered financial losses and penalties, but are also fearful of reputational damage. Forty-seven percent of surveyed SOEs report financial losses as a result of corruption and other irregular practices, amounting to an average loss of 1.4% of annual corporate profits (including cost estimates relating to compliance with enforcement actions or sanctions that have been paid). Moreover, in establishing prevention and detection mechanisms, SOEs were more motivated by a fear of reputational damage, enforcement or divestment by broader investors (non-state), than by risk of legal or enforcement actions by shareholders. For SOEs that are not listed, and have a larger share of SOE ownership, attention may be paid to the "too public to fail" mentality, where SOEs feel insulated from legal or enforcement action.

SOEs could consult the US' Department of Justice (DoJ) "Evaluation of Corporate Compliance Programs" (2017) which is a valuable tool for reflecting on the strength of the SOEs' integrity mechanisms in face of suspected misconduct. As an indication of the types of questions that are asked in evaluations by the DoJ, it is not meant to be a check-the-box list of items. It too should be tailored to an individual company. It can effectively enable SOEs to reverse engineer their integrity and anti-corruption programmes. Examples of these questions that can be used to assess the strength of a company's response and improvement in face of corruption allegations are provided in Box 2.13.

Box 2.13. Key questions to assess companies' capacity for adequate response, prevention and improvement in cases of non-compliance

Evolving Updates – How often has the company updated its risk assessments and reviewed its compliance policies, procedures, and practices? What steps has the company taken to determine whether policies/procedures/practices make sense for particular business segments/subsidiaries?

Remediation – What specific changes has the company made to reduce the risk that the same or similar issues will not occur in the future? What specific remediation has addressed the issues identified in the root cause and missed opportunity analysis?

Root Cause Analysis – What is the company's root cause analysis of the misconduct at issue? What systemic issues were identified? Who in the company was involved in making the analysis?

Prior Indications – Were there prior opportunities to detect the misconduct in question, such as audit reports identifying relevant control failures or allegations, complaints, or investigations involving similar issues? What is the company's analysis of why such opportunities were missed?

Source: United States' Government, Department of Justice (2017), "Evaluation of Corporate Compliance Programs", www.justice.gov/criminal-fraud/page/file/937501/download.

Notes

[1] For more information, please see page 90 of OECD (2015a), Corporate Governance and Business Integrity: A Stocktaking of Corporate Practices, , www.oecd.org/daf/ca/Corporate-Governance-Business-Integrity-2015.pdf

[2] The correlation included 27 of the countries participating in the SOE survey. Data was not available for Iceland, Israel, Latvia, Lithuania, Pakistan, Slovakia or Switzerland.

[3] Out of the 197 valid company responses available for this question, 104 companies reported not losing a share of annual corporate profits to rule-breaking and corruption (including cost estimates relating to compliance with enforcement actions or sanctions that have been paid). The remaining 93 companies (47%) had at least one respondent within the company estimate losing profits.

[4] Article 8 of the 2009 Anti-Bribery Recommendation, section X (accounting, external audit, internal controls, ethics and compliance) and Annex II, Good Practice Guidance, sub-section 7.

[5] The Financial Action Task Force provides Guidance on Politically Exposed Persons, www.fatf-gafi.org/media/fatf/documents/recommendations/Guidance-PEP-Rec12-22.pdf.

[6] Ethisphere's "World's Most Ethical Companies Honoree List" compiles companies recognized for their critical role to drive positive change in their business committee and around the world. In 2018, 135 companies from 23 countries and 57 industries are featured on the list, available here: www.worldsmostethicalcompanies.com/honorees.

[7] See OECD's "Preventing Corruption in Public Procurement" for examples of utilisation of "integrity pacts", www.oecd.org/gov/ethics/Corruption-in-Public-Procurement-Brochure.pdf.

[8] This may occur in instances where there is a state warranty on defined liabilities of SOEs or contributions collected by means of taxation for special activities run by the enterprise.

[9] MNEs observed more misconduct in the previous 12 months (36%) compared to domestic companies (29%) but were slightly less likely to report it at 59% versus reporting of domestic companies at 60%. In both types of companies, those reporting misconduct experienced retaliation – 35% in domestic and 32% in MNEs. Rate of misconduct is higher in companies that operate in more than one country (ECI, 2016).

[10] Thirty-eight percent of respondents of companies that are suppliers personally observed misconduct in the previous 12 months, versus 27% who did not. Sixty-six percent of suppliers reported observing misconduct, while 54% of non-suppliers did not. Companies that are suppliers were also more likely to experience retaliation for reporting misconduct (39%) versus non-suppliers (27%) (ECI, 2016).

References

ACLEI (2017), Australian Commission for Law Enforcement Integrity, www.aclei.gov.au/corruption-prevention/key-concepts/values-alignment.

ACFE (2016), *Report to the Nations on Occupational Fraud and Abuse*, 2016 Global Fraud Survey, Association of Certified Fraud Examiners, www.acfe.com/rttn2016/docs/2016-report-to-the-nations.pdf.

Australian Government Department of Finance (2017), *Benchmarking Survey 2017 – Risk Management Maturity Capability Levels*, www.finance.gov.au/sites/default/files/rm-capability-maturity-levels-2017.pdf

Control Risks (2017), International Business Attitudes to Compliance, Report 2017, https://www.controlrisks.com/our-thinking/insights/reports/international-business-attitudes-to-compliance.

COSO (2017), Enterprise Risk Management: integrating with strategy and performance, Executive Summary, Committee of Sponsoring Organizations of the Treadway Commission, www.coso.org/Pages/default.asp.

Department of Justice, United States (2017), "Evaluation of Corporate Compliance Programs", www.justice.gov/criminal-fraud/page/file/937501/download.

Deloitte (2014), Director 360: Growth from all directions, www2.deloitte.com/content/dam/Deloitte/global/Documents/Risk/gx-ccg-director-360-growth-from-all-directions-third-edition.pdf.

ECI (2016), *Measuring Risk and Promoting Workplace Integrity, Global Business Ethics Survey*, Ethics and Compliance Initiative, 2016, www.ethics.org/ecihome/research/gbes/gbes-form.

EY (2016), Corporate misconduct – individual consequences: Global enforcement focuses the spotlight on executive integrity, Ernst & Young, www.ey.com/Publication/vwLUAssets/EY-corporate-misconduct-individual-consequences/USDFILE/EY-corporate-misconduct-individual-consequences.pdf.

FATF (2013), FATF Guidance: Politically Exposed Persons (Recommendations 12 and 22), Financial Action Task Force, www.fatf-gafi.org/media/fatf/documents/recommendations/Guidance-PEP-Rec12-22.pdf.

FSB (2017), Stocktake of efforts to strengthen governance frameworks to mitigate misconduct risks, Financial Stability Board, www.fsb.org/2017/05/stocktake-of-efforts-to-strengthen-governance-frameworks-to-mitigate-misconduct-risks/.

G20 (2015), G20 High-Level Principles on Private Sector Transparency and Integrity, http://g20.org.tr/wp-content/uploads/2015/11/G20-High-Level-Principles-on-Private-Sector-Transparency-and-Integrity.pdf.

Georgetown University (2017), Impact, Likelihood and Velocity, https://riskmanagement.georgetown.edu/RiskAssessmentMeasures.

IMF, (2017), *The Role of the Fund in Governance Issues - Review of the Guidance Note - Preliminary Considerations - Background Notes*, Policy Papers, International Monetary Fund, www.imf.org/en/Publications/Policy-Papers/Issues/2017/08/01/pp080217-background-notes-the-role-of-the-fund-in-governance-issues-review-of-the-guidance-note

ISO 37001 (2016), "Anti-bribery management systems -- Requirements with guidance for use", International Organization for Standardization, hwww.iso.org/standard/65034.html

OECD (2018), *Behavioural Insights for Public Integrity: Harnessing the Human Factor to Counter Corruption*, OECD Public Governance Reviews, OECD Publishing, Paris, www.oecd.org/gov/ethics/behavioural-insights-for-public-integrity-9789264297067-en.htm.

OECD (2017a), *The Detection of Foreign Bribery,* OECD Publishing, Paris, www.oecd.org/corruption/the-detection-of-foreign-bribery.htm.

OECD (2017b), *OECD Integrity Review of Colombia: Investing in Integrity for Peace and Prosperity*, OECD Publishing, Paris, http://dx.doi.org/10.1787/9789264278325-en.

OECD (2016a), *Checklist for Supporting the Implementation of the OECD Recommendation of the Council on Public Procurement*, www.oecd.org/governance/procurement/toolbox/search/checklist-implementation-oecd-recommendation.pdf.

OECD (2016b), *Committing to Effective Whistleblower Protection*, OECD Publishing, Paris, www.oecd.org/corporate/committing-to-effective-whistleblower-protection-9789264252639-en.htm.

OECD (2016c), *Liability of Legal Persons for Foreign Bribery: A Stocktaking Report,* OECD Publishing, www.oecd.org/corruption/liability-of-legal-persons-for-foreign-bribery-stocktaking-report.htm

OECD (2015a), *Corporate Governance and Business Integrity: A stocktaking of Corporate Practices,* www.oecd.org/corruption/corporate-governance-business-integrity-stocktaking-corporate-practices.htm.

OECD (2015b), *OECD Guidelines on Corporate Governance of State-Owned Enterprises,* 2015 Edition, OECD Publishing, Paris, www.oecd.org/corporate/guidelines-corporate-governance-soes.htm.

OECD (2014), *OECD Foreign Bribery Report: An Analysis of the Crime of Bribery of Foreign Public Officials*, OECD Publishing, Paris, www.oecd.org/corruption/oecd-foreign-bribery-report-9789264226616-en.htm.

OECD (2010), Good Practice Guidance on Internal Controls, Ethics, and Compliance, www.oecd.org/daf/anti-bribery/44884389.pdf.

OECD (2013), OECD/UNODC/World Bank, *Anti-Corruption Ethics and Compliance Handbook for Business*, www.oecd.org/corruption/anti-corruption-ethics-and-compliance-handbook-for-business.htm.

PwC (2016a), *Adjusting the Lens on Economic Crime: Preparation brings opportunity back into focus,* Global Economic Crime Survey 2016, Price Waterhouse Coopers, www.pwc.com/gx/en/economic-crime-survey/pdf/GlobalEconomicCrimeSurvey2016.pdf.

PwC (2011), Fighting Fraud in the Public Sector, www.pwc.com/gx/en/psrc/pdf/fighting_fraud_in_the_public_sector_june2011.pdf

TI (2017), 10 Anti-Corruption Principles for State-Owned Enterprises, Transparency International, www.transparency.org/whatwedo/tools/10_anti_corruption_principles/0.

Transparency International et al. (2013), *Business Principles for Countering Bribery,* www.transparency.org/whatwedo/tools/business_principles_for_countering_bribery/1.

Transparency International UK (2012), *The 2010 UK Bribery Act Adequate Procedures Checklist*, Transparency International UK, London, 2010, www.transparency.org.uk/publications/adequate-procedures-checklist-pdf/#.W0Yf-tIzbcs.

UN (2005), United Nations Convention Against Corruption, United Nations, New York, 2004, www.unodc.org/unodc/en/treaties/CAC/.

US Department of Justice (2017) "Evaluation of Corporate Compliance Programs", www.justice.gov/criminal-fraud/page/file/937501/download.

World Bank Group (2010), Integrity Compliance Guidelines, World Bank, Washington DC, http://siteresources.worldbank.org/INTDOII/Resources/Integrity_Compliance_Guidelines.pdf.

World Economic Forum (2016), *Partnering Against Corruption Initiative: Principles for Countering Bribery, Multinational Task Force*, www3.weforum.org/docs/WEF_PACI_Global_Principles_for_Countering_Corruption.pdf.

WJP (2017), World Justice Project Rule of Law Index 2017-2018, World Justice Project, worldjusticeproject.org/our-work/wjp-rule-law-index/wjp-rule-law-index-2017%E2%80%932018.

Annex 2.A. List of obstacles in the OECD state-owned enterprise survey

Table 2.A1.1: Obstacles to integrity: Question options from the state-owned enterprise survey

Response options for the following question: in your opinion, to what degree does each factor pose as an obstacle to effectively promoting integrity and preventing corruption in, or involving, your company?

List of obstacles put forth to SOE respondents to rank each: very much an obstacle, an obstacle, somewhat an obstacle, not at all an obstacle, NA/does not exist
Obstacles regarding relations with government
A lack of a culture of integrity in the political and public sector
Overly complex or burdensome legal requirements
Relations between your company, or the board, and political officials
Obstacles regarding company culture
A lack of a culture of integrity in your company
A lack of awareness among employees of the need for, or priority placed on, integrity
A lack of awareness of legal requirements
Conflicting corporate objectives
Inadequate financial or human resources to invest in integrity and anti-corruption
Inadequate remuneration/compensation
Loyalty to company
Loyalty to customers or third parties
Unsupportive leadership from the Board or management
Penalisation of whistleblowers/reporting
Pressure to perform or meet targets
Pressure to rule-break
Obstacles regarding controls and accountability
Ineffective channels for whistleblowing / reporting misconduct
Ineffective internal audit
Ineffective external audit
Ineffective internal control or risk management
Unclear or ineffective reporting lines between integrity units and Board
Unclear or ineffective reporting lines between Board and others
Obstacles regarding behaviour
Perceived cost of corruption is low and/or return is high
Perceived likelihood of getting caught is low
Opportunistic behaviour of individuals

Source: OECD 2017 Survey of anti-corruption and integrity in SOEs

Chapter 3. The state as an active and informed owner: What can and should it do?

This chapter offers the state as owner a range of policy responses to the key challenges to SOE integrity identified in chapters 1 and 2. Informed by consultation with 28 state ownership entities, it provides a comparison of broad policy and regulatory frameworks that SOEs are subject to with regards to integrity and anti-corruption and the variety of supporting activities that state ownership entities undertake. Ownership entities are encouraged to consider the adequacy of their existing approaches, capacity and the state's own integrity to be active, professional, accountable and transparent owners, and to lead by example.

Overview: The state as an active and informed owner

This section summarises and highlights the main findings from the remainder of the chapter, which analyses the contributions of government officials in 28 countries describing their national practices toward promoting integrity and fighting corruption in and around SOEs (Annex B). State ownership responses mostly take the national legal framework applicable to SOEs as given. In consequence responses systematically differ between countries whose SOEs mostly take the form of joint stock companies subject to ordinary corporate legislation and those whose SOEs are largely subject to public law.

The SOE survey showed that corporate insiders consider that the legal and regulatory framework for anti-corruption and integrity is clearly laid out on paper, but they see an issue with the awareness and implementation of it throughout the SOE hierarchy. There is also a lack of understanding of their importance of integrity. States may consider strengthening the following approaches based on SOEs' risks of corruption and obstacles to integrity, and based on existing good practices to minimise them:

- **Leading by example with regards to integrity and accountability**. SOEs perceive that a lack of integrity in the public sector is one of the main obstacles to promoting integrity and preventing and detecting corruption in their SOE. Measures must be established to counter any existing incentives for the state or state actors to hide corruption or other irregular practices in the interest of corporate insiders or policy makers.
- **Ensuring a level playing field by making SOE objectives, and any subsidies or preferential treatment, transparent.** Companies with mixed objectives (public policy and commercial) report less corruption than companies with entirely commercial objectives, but face influence in decision-making and higher risks than entirely commercial companies. A high-level of disclosure should be required for SOES with public policy objectives, yet SOEs with entirely commercial objectives report to disclose financial assistance slightly more often than SOEs with policy objectives, suggesting a greater need for transparency in the ownership and financial assistance to SOEs pursuing policy objectives. There is potential that SOEs with mixed objectives under reported the degree to which they have witnessed corrupt or other irregular practices in recent years.
- **Making expectations about anti-corruption and integrity explicit as part of their broader expectations for SOEs, and actively communicating them**. Four out of five survey respondents felt state expectations around anti-corruption and integrity were clearly communicated by the state – the rest were more likely to have seen corruption risks materialise in their companies in recent years. Good practices in communicating state expectations include specific references in ownership policies, ownership initiatives on the subject, exposure and awareness of government-wide anti-corruption initiatives, dissemination through regular meetings and trainings, at least at board level, and issuing supporting guidance on implementation.
- **Contributing to well-informed, objective and autonomous boards**. Evidence shows that companies with a higher proportion of independents (non-executive and non-state) on the board, and a lower proportion of state representatives, is associated with a lower risk of corruption and other irregular practices.
- **Encouraging more inclusive and annual assessments of corruption risks within the SOE that are regularly presented to and deliberated by the board**. The state should define and communicate a broad classification of corruption risks that are

considered important and should thus be shared with the state ownership entity. Chapter 1 showed the diversity of risk perceptions, often dependent upon position, role and status of the respondent, putting emphasis on the need for more inclusive risk assessments and for more systematic communication between integrity functions and the board. Boards are not always provided with relevant integrity and risk findings and, when they are, some SOEs pointed to a lack of their deliberation by the board. Finally, only 34% of companies publicly disclose material foreseeable risk factors and measures taken to manage such risks. The state ownership entity may also consider channels to be regularly informed about corruption risks, and to develop a capacity to better understand them.

- **Developing consistent procedures when notified of cases of actual or suspected corruption**. In most countries there is no systematic approach by the ownership entity to deal with corruption suspicions. It is done in an ad-hoc manner that suggests states could benefit from a clearer plan of action, including requiring adequate follow-up from the SOE that takes into account the potential roles of the ownership entity, regulatory authorities, enforcement agencies and the Supreme Audit Institution. Meeting opportunistic behaviour or undue influence in SOEs with strict enforcement will demonstrate that the SOEs do not unfairly benefit from their state ownership, market position or role in pursuing policy objectives.

Improving effectiveness and accountability of the state

The second chapter of the SOE Guidelines focuses on the state fulfilling a role as an informed and active owner, ensuring that the governance of SOEs is carried out in a transparent and accountable manner and with a high degree of professionalism and effectiveness. The ownership entity – charged with exercising the ownership rights of the state – is given primary responsibility for this and must have adequate skills and resources to oversee the performance of the SOE, including the adequacy of anti-corruption and integrity mechanisms.

Promoting transparency and accountability of SOEs is not just a job for the ownership entity but requires governments to lead by example in good governance and ethical conduct, and in their enforcement. It requires a whole-of-government approach, as promoted in OECD's 2017 Recommendation of the Council on Public Integrity (OECD, 2017a). According to the survey of SOE officials, a lack of integrity in the public sector is one of the foremost obstacles to integrity in their companies. The challenge stems not only from direct undue influence or involvement in SOEs, through membership in the board or third-party interactions in procurement, for instance, but also indirectly where weak detection and enforcement leaves SOEs vulnerable or opportunistic.

There is a chain of actors responsible for ensuring anti-corruption and integrity in SOEs. The government ownership entity may or may not see itself as an explicit part, but government should set the tone for integrity and ethics, and consider how to address the issues that SOEs have raised. In addition, state ownership entities should continue striving to adhere to the SOE Guidelines (2015a)

Protecting integrity in SOEs is not only about the integrity of individuals serving on boards or within the state ownership entity, but the public sector and its officials and employees across the board. Efforts of SOEs, or those responsible for exercising ownership on behalf of the state (ownership entities or line ministries), cannot be undermined by their colleagues' lack of integrity.

Improving government integrity requires a whole of government approach and strong democratic institutions. Potential for co-ordination between relevant authorities to promote integrity across the entire government apparatus is covered below.

As outlined in the OECD's Public Integrity recommendation (2017b), a culture of integrity in the public sector is fostered through high standards of conduct for public officials, communicating public sector values and standards internally in public sector organisations and externally to the private sector, civil society and individuals, and asking these partners to respect those values and standards in their interactions with public officials (OECD, 2017a).

Bolstering state ownership entities' capacities in the area of anti-corruption and integrity

The ownership entity should develop consistent reporting on SOEs and publish an aggregate report on SOEs annually. The ownership entity is reliant on the quality and accuracy of inputs from SOE boards, or management reporting via the boards, on the efficiency and effectiveness of internal audit, competencies, objective reasoning, an understanding of what is material by the board and the quality of external auditors.

In view of the above findings of corruption in SOEs, as well as the variance in risk perceptions, ownership entities may wish to develop capacities to assess the reliability of reporting and understand any red flags brought to its attention. Related, ownership entities may also wish to develop adequate accounting and audit competencies to ensure sufficient communication with relevant counterparts, both with SOEs' financial services, its internal audit function and specific state controllers.

Some ownership entities have the capacities and skill-sets to identify risks, including corruption risks, directly. Developing capacity for integrity, anti-corruption, compliance, corporate social responsibility, or responsible business conduct requires time and resources.

In some countries related skills are developed within the ownership entity itself, as has been done in Norway for instance, where the ownership entity has developed skills to assess anti-corruption and integrity, built up through other initiatives and through learning opportunities in engaging third parties, such as PwC, on the subject. In the Philippines' Governance Commission for Government-Owned or Government Controlled Corporations (GCG), lawyers are trained on whistleblowing and investigations. One of the first trainings that staff of the Treasury of the Polish Chancellery receives is in anti-corruption.

Ownership entities could also establish a legal unit to consult on related matters as is done by the French authority, l'Agence des participations de l'État (APE), to consult on matters related to conflict of interest. Other countries may rely on independent groups to advise. In Iceland, the Ministry of Finance (the state ownership entity) appoints members to the independent Complaints Board for Public Procurement, which also applies to complaints against SOEs. While the Ministry of Finance does not hire for specific skills sets, it sees its representatives as having the necessary combined skills.

In yet other countries, ownership entities do not hire for specific skills sets, instead relying on the monitoring function of other state authorities, such as the Supreme Audit Institution, as is the case of Switzerland.

Co-ordinating with other relevant state authorities for improved anti-corruption and integrity in state-owned enterprises

The SOE Guidelines posit that, when appropriate and permitted by the legal system and the state's level of ownership, a primary responsibility of the ownership entity is to maintain continuous dialogue with external auditors and specific state control organs (OECD, 2015a: II.F.6.).

The relationship of the ownership entity with other government bodies should be clearly defined (II.E). A number of state bodies, ministries or administrations may have different roles vis-à-vis the same SOEs. In order to increase public confidence in the way the state manages ownership of SOEs, it is important that these different roles be clearly identified and explained to the general public. For instance, the ownership entity should maintain co-operation and continuous dialogue with the SAIs responsible for auditing the SOEs.

The role of the state ownership entity should be given sufficient autonomy from other roles of the state – notably regulatory policy. As such, some countries co-ordinate only in the context of specific investigations if at all.

The majority of 28 state ownership entities that contributed directly to this report have some level of co-ordination and interaction with relevant authorities. Most often this is ad-hoc or "as needed". Country experiences reported by state ownership entities outline the myriad of benefits that can come from professional co-ordination between relevant authorities. A company in New Zealand reported that one way in which the ownership entity supports them in anti-corruption and integrity is in networking across other Government Agencies. In the Czech Republic, the Minister of Finance coordinates through the Minister for Human Rights, Equal Opportunities and Legislation and Chair of the Government Anti-Corruption Coordination Council under the Prime Minister's office.

Based on the national responses to the questionnaire, benefits of professional, cross-governmental co-ordination include the following:

- Staying well informed: State ownership entities may supply relevant information to authorities that may be required for investigations, annual reports or commentary on a specific risk, activity or sector. They may also demand such information in order to stay abreast of commentaries of SOE performance and conduct, such as audit reports for follow-up with companies. In view of the above findings, ownership entities can co-ordinate to be better informed about corruption vulnerabilities – such as ineffective internal controls - and their impact on performance.
- Co-operating with relevant authorities for investigations and enforcement, as needed and as discussed in section 3.6. The Polish authority co-ordinates with regulatory agencies on regular basis tailored to needs, answers questions and submits materials to administrative courts.
- Providing anti-corruption and integrity requirements and guidance, such as jointly developing a compliance programme with capacity building component; issuing guidelines for implementation of related legislation by SOEs or establishing recommendations for how the board and management of SOEs can put into place related mechanisms
  - Italy's Ministry of Finance, exercising state ownership, has a long history in co-ordinating with the Italian National Anti-Corruption Agency (ANAC). Such co-operation has led to issuance of formal rules and binding mechanisms to prevent corruption. According to ANAC, each SOE is asked to identify the

"Responsible for preventing corruption" in its company and the person is appointed by the board of directors, with main area of responsibility consisting of drafting the action plan to tackle both illegal and hidden behaviour that could be put into practice by managers and employees. Finally, this plan must be adopted by the board of directors.

- In Brazil, the 2016 normative instruction issued by the Ministry of Transparency (CGU) and the Ministry of Planning sought to strengthen internal controls and risk management of predominantly public entities. Further, Secretariat of Coordination and Governance (SEST) has informal discussions about corporate governance issues with relevant authorities in Brazil as needed.

Disseminating state expectations for anti-corruption and integrity

Legal and regulatory frameworks for anti-corruption and integrity

An SOE is any corporate entity recognised by national law as an enterprise and in which the state has majority ownership, or otherwise is able to exercise control (OECD, 2015). This includes joint-stock companies, limited liability companies, partnerships limited by shares, as well as statutory corporations if their purpose and activities are largely of an economic nature. The legal functions of SOEs – ranging from primarily governmental to primarily commercial – impacts the level of corporatisation[1] of an SOE and thus the legal and regulatory framework which underpins the execution of said functions. Useful information about the form of SOEs is found in *The Size and Sectoral Distribution of State-Owned Enterprises* (OECD, 2017b).

Another OECD study of 33 OECD member and partner countries showed the majority of SOEs as having the same legal form as private companies, generally subjecting them to commercial laws (Figure 3.1). However, countries may additionally, or instead, establish SOE-specific laws for certain or for all SOEs or apply various public laws with thematic relevance to its SOEs (e.g. public procurement, public employment or public financial management). SOEs may also be subject to requirements found in state ownership policies, guidelines or codes.

Figure 3.1 shows that 24% of surveyed[2] countries have SOEs with predominantly distinct legal forms, such as statutory corporations, or SOE-specific legislation. Distinct legal personalities should be reserved for corporations largely operating with a public policy function: such forms are not desirable for public enterprises that have purely commercial objectives and that operate in competitive and open markets (OECD, 2005; 2015). SOEs that are given public policy objectives may benefit from the protection of a distinct public service role in order to deliver on those policy objectives in an efficient and effective manner. This protection could include protection from insolvency, and protection with regard to regulated remuneration and pensions.

SOEs excluded from the application of certain legislation, or are given a distinct legal personality, should not preclude clear and transparent demarcation of an SOEs' activities and ability to expand the scope of operations overseas or to new sectors. Further, it should be accompanied by high standards for accountability and disclosure such that SOEs with policy objectives do not negate responsibilities to shareholders and to the public (OECD, 2015a). As shown above, SOEs established by statutory legislation can be subject to company law or SOE-specific rules.

Figure 3.1. Legal forms of state-owned enterprises and applicability of commercial law

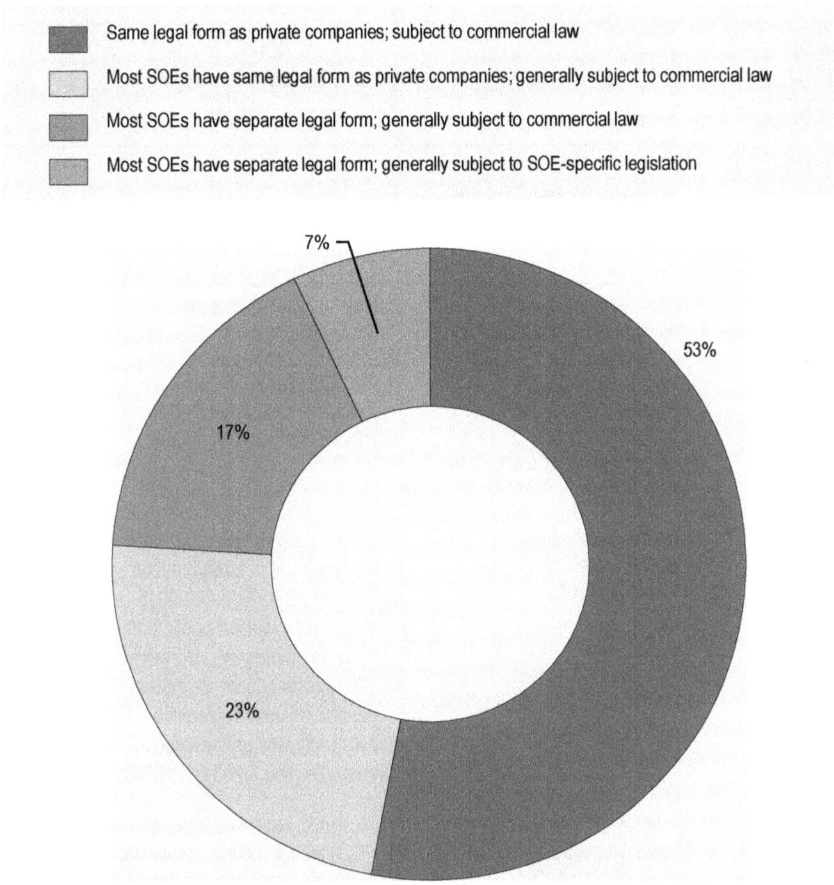

Note: Based on responses to the July 2016 Risk Management Questionnaire of the Working Party on State Ownership and Privatisation Practices, as well as the reponses from the 29 countries represented in the OECD 2017 Survey of anti-corruption and integrity in SOEs. It also includes Austria, Belgium, Germany, Ireland, Israel, Japan, Kazakhstan, Lithuania, New Zealand, Portugal, Slovenia, Spain and the United Kingdom. It does not include Canada or Colombia.

Source: OECD (2016a), *Risk Management by State-Owned Enterprises and their Ownership*, OECD Publishing, Paris. http://dx.doi.org/10.1787/9789264262249-en.

Table 3.1 provides an overview of select legal provisions for anti-corruption and integrity in the legal and regulatory frameworks of the 28 countries participating in this ownership questionnaire. The provisions are based on self-reporting without an independent or comprehensive analysis of country laws, and they do not include criminal laws.

All countries, except the Philippines, apply a commercial law. All countries have established additional provisions applying to SOEs, whether SOE-specific policies, codes or guidelines or thematically-relevant public laws. Provisions related to anti-corruption and integrity are stratified across these documents.

Mechanisms for their implementation and enforcement differ widely, with some being merely advisory, others being implemented (by stock markets or securities regulators) on a comply-or-explain basis, and yet others being mandatory. For instance, regulations on whistleblowing or lobbying are recommended by the ownership entity for SOEs but are not binding.

Table 3.1. Overview of countries legal and regulatory framework for anti-corruption and integrity in state-owned enterprises

Country	legal form: Incorporated using same legal from as private firms in like circumstances (P) or Statutory (S) / Application of commercial law (C)	ACI-related provisions found in:	
		SOE-specific laws, policies, codes or guidelines	Additional public laws applicable to SOEs (other than criminal law)
Argentina	S / C	Decree 606/2012 – "Transparency Provisions for listed enterprises"; SIGEN Regulation 37/2006 – "Principles of Internal Control for Good Corporate Governance of SOEs" (not for listed SOEs)	Decree 1172/2003 "Disclosure of Management of Interests in the Public Sector"; Law 27.275 - "Access to Information Law"; Decree 202/2017 – "Conflict of Interests in Procurement"; Public Ethics Law 25188; Anticorruption Office Resolution 11- E/2017 "Conflict of Interests in Procurement"; Decree 1179/2016 – "Gift regulations for public officials"
Brazil	S / C	Law on Responsibility of Federal State Companies - Law 13.303/2016	Sanctions (Law 8.429/1992); Law 12.846/2013 (liability for acts against national or foreign public administration, including leniency agreement); Decree 8.420/2015 (administrative responsibility of legal entities of acts against public administration); Ordinance 909/2015 (evaluation of integrity programmes of legal entities); Ordinance 910/2015 (procedures for determining administrative responsibility);Joint Normative ruling 1/2016 (internal controls, risk management and governance standards); Law 12.813 (conflict of interest); Decree 7.203 (prohibition of nepotism); .
Canada**	*	Governance Framework Crown Corporations (Financial Administration Act)	COIA, Public sector disclosure protection act; value and ethics code for PS; rules for federal political donations; lobbying act; Open and Accountable Government (Annex A for public office holders, as defined in conflict of interest act); Integrity Regime (all departments and agencies, administered by public services and procurement Canada - CCs encouraged to adopt on a VOLUNTARY basis); Corruption of foreign public officials act (applicable to public officials generally including all CCs)
Chile	P / C	Corporate Governance Guidelines	Board Members and executive management as Politically Exposed Persons (aw 19.913 makes BMs and executive management PEPs); declaration of interest / patrimony each year for board members and managers); Lobbying (where state is the major shareholder meetings with third parties must be disclosed)
Colombia	*	Law 489 – 2011	Law 1474 – 2011 Decree 4632 - 2011 Decree 734 -2012 Law 1712 – 2014 Decree 103 – 2015
Czech Republic	P / C	Law No. 106/1999 Coll., on Free Access to Information; Law No. 340/2015 Coll., the Contract Register Act	Law No. 234/2014 Coll., as amended, on Civil Service; n 2017 the law amending the Act No. 159/2006 Coll., on Conflict of Interest, was ratified; Action Plan of the Czech Republic - Open Government Partnership for 2016 to 2018; Anti-Corruption Action Plan for 2016 of the Czech Government

Country	legal form: Incorporated using same legal from as private firms in like circumstances (P) or Statutory (S) / Application of commercial law (C)	ACI-related provisions found in:	
		SOE-specific laws, policies, codes or guidelines	Additional public laws applicable to SOEs (other than criminal law)
Denmark	P / C	"Staten som aktionær (2004)" (The state as shareholder) and "Statens ejerskabspolitik (2015)" (The states ownership-policy)	
Finland	P / C	Government resolution on state-ownership policy - 13.5.2016; State Shareholding and Ownership Steering Act.	Public Procurement (1397/2016)
France	P / C		Annual Financial Reports for companies in extractive, exploitative, or forest industries (additional requirements based on EU law); (Anti-Money Laundering and Anti-Terrorist Financing: n° 2016-1635 2016); Public Procurement (n° 2014/24/UE et 2014/25/UE); Law on Transparency, Fight on Corruption and Modernisation of the Economy (n°2016-1691 2016)
Greece	P / C	"SOEs Legal Framework" - Law 3429/05	
Hungary	*	Act. No. CXXII of 2009. on the more economical functioning of public companies	370/2011. (31 Dec.) Government Decree On the internal control system and internal control of budgetary organs ; The National Anti-Corruption Program and related Actions 2015-2016. 1336/2015 on the adoption of the plan for the year; (V.27) Government Decision 50/2013. (II.25.) Government decree The system of integrity management of the state administration bodies and the order of receiving advocates Government Decision No. 1239/2017. (IV.28.) on measures related to the National Anti-Corruption Program 2017-2018.
Iceland	P / C	Ownership policies for SOEs - one for financial services SOEs and one general policy for all SOEs	Some specific clauses in the laws pertaining to limited liability companies and annual accounts that apply to all companies, including SOEs, which address the issue of internal control and risk management. More stringent such regulations apply to financial services companies, implemented from EU laws/regulations
Italy	P / C		Guidelines of the Italian Anti-Corruption Authority (ANAC) (2014, updated in 2017 by ANAC Resolution 1134/2017) in addition to those formally laid out in Legislative Decree n. 231/2001
Japan	S / C	SOE-specific laws for statutory SOEs	Like other public companies, listed SOE has to be audited by external accounting auditors
Kazakhstan	*		Provisions in the Law of the Republic of Kazakhstan "on Joint-Stock companies" (2003) and "On limited and additional liability partnerships" (1998); as well as Law "On Combatting Corruption" of 18 November 2015; Code of the Republic of Kazakhstan "On Administrative Offences" of 5 July 2014 there is a liability for violations of the legislation on government procurement

Country	legal form: Incorporated using same legal from as private firms in like circumstances (P) or Statutory (S) / Application of commercial law (C)	ACI-related provisions found in:	
		SOE-specific laws, policies, codes or guidelines	Additional public laws applicable to SOEs (other than criminal law)
Korea	*	Provisions in management of public institutions; management of public corporations; budget execution; HR management ; performance evaluation	Act on the Prevention of Corruption and the Establishment and Management of the Anti-Corruption and Civil Rights Commission; Improper Solicitation and Graft Act
Latvia	P / C		Law on Governance of Capital Shares of a public person and Capital Companies; Law on Prevention of Conflict of Interest in Activities of Public Officials; state administration structure law; Government regulation on nomination of executive board and supervisory board
Mexico	S / C	SOE-specific laws for statutory SOEs	General Law of the National Anticorruption System (Ley General del Sistema Nacional Anticorrupción – LGSNA); General Law on Administrative Responsibilites (Ley General de Responsabilidades Administrativas – LGRA)
Netherlands	P / C	Corporate Governance Code; Ownership internal policy	Anti-Money Laundering and Anti-Terrorist financing
Norway	P / C	Meld. St. 27 (2013-2014) Report to the Storting (white paper) Corporate Governance Code (for listed companies, on comply or explain basis);	Procurement Law (applicable to SOEs that serve the general public and are not of an industrial or business character);
Paraguay	*	Code of Corporate Governance (Decree N ° 6381/2016)	Applying to SOEs: remuneration (Law No. 5189/2014); Law No. 5282/2014 and Decree No. 4064/2015 (access to information); Decree No. 4900/2016 (National Plan for Anti-Corruption)
Peru	*	Code of Corporate Governance; Conduct and Ethics Guidelines ; Transparency Guidelines (for enterprises under FONAFE supervision)	Law 28716 on the Internal Control System of State Entities; Law 30225 on Government Procurement; Law 30294; Law 29622 on Decentralisation; Whistleblower protection (Law 29542 and Decree-Law 1327); Access to Public Information (Law 1353)
Philippines	S	GOCC Governance Act of 2011 (Republic Act No. 10149)	Code of Conduct and Ethics Standards for public officials and employees; Procurement Law
Poland	P / C	Law of 16 December 2016 - rules of state property management ; Good Practices of companies listed on the Warsaw Stock Exchange; Law of 9 June 2016 about the principles of shaping the remuneration of managers of some companies	Law of 9 June 2006 on the Central Anticorruption Bureau; Law of 15 September 2000 Code of Commercial Companies
Slovenia	P / C	Companies Act, Corporate Governance Code	The Slovenian Sovereign Holding (SSH) Act, Chapter 6***
Sweden	P / C	Corporate Governance Code (for listed companies, with a	Procurement Law (applicable to SOEs receiving funds from state for public policy objectives); Swedish Transparency Act (for those

Country	legal form: Incorporated using same legal from as private firms in like circumstances (P) or Statutory (S) / Application of commercial law (C)	ACI-related provisions found in:	
		SOE-specific laws, policies, codes or guidelines	Additional public laws applicable to SOEs (other than criminal law)
		few exceptions, on comply or explain basis); State Ownership Policy	receiving funds from state or other benefits from the state, or those reaching a certain level of sales - based on EU transparency rules)
Switzerland	P / C		Regarding internal control (Art. 728a Swiss Code of Obligations; SR 220) and risk management (Art 961c Swiss Code of Obligations; SR 220); public procurement rules
Turkey	P / C	Decree Law Nr:233	No 5176 Public Ethic Law; No: 5018 Public Financial Management and Financial Control Law.; No: 4734 Public Procurement Law.; No: 4982 Right of Information Acquirement.; No: 5176 Establishment of Council of Ethics for Public Officials; No: 2499 Turkish Capital Markets Board Article 47, Administrative Pecuniary Punishments for insider trading.; Prevention of Transfer of Funds From Public Institutions to Foundations/Associations; No: 5549 Prevention of Laundering Proceeds of Crime; No: 6328 Establishment on the Ombudsman; Law No: 3628 Declaration of Assets.

Notes: It is a basic premise of the SOE Guidelines that SOEs should be subject to best practice governance standards of listed enterprises. This implies that both listed and unlisted SOEs should always comply with the national corporate governance code, irrespectively of how "binding" they are; * Information missing; ** Refers only to SOEs at the Federal level, referred to as Crown Corporations; *** Chapter 6: "M*easures to enhance integrity and responsibility and limitation of risks of corruption, conflict of interest and abuse of internal information in the management of assets of the state*". P = Most SOEs in the jurisdiction are incorporated using same legal from as private firms in like circumstances; S = Most SOEs in the jurisdiction are statutory or quasi-corporations. C = SOEs are generally subject to company law.

Source: OECD 2017 Survey of anti-corruption and integrity in SOEs; OECD (2017d), *The Size and Sectoral Distribution of State-Owned Enterprises*, OECD Publishing, Paris. http://dx.doi.org/10.1787/9789264280663-en; OECD (2016b), "The ownership and governance of state-owned enterprises", in *State-Owned Enterprises as Global Competitors: A Challenge or an Opportunity?*, OECD Publishing, Paris. http://dx.doi.org/10.1787/9789264262096-9-en; OECD (2016a), Risk Management by State-Owned Enterprises and their Ownership, OECD Publishing, Paris. http://dx.doi.org/10.1787/9789264262249-en.

Clarifying state expectations around anti-corruption and integrity

When SOE respondents were asked how clearly, in their assessment, "relevant national laws, regulations, bylaws or governance codes establish expectations and requirements for their company's actions and responsibilities in the areas of integrity and anti-corruption (including for internal control, risk management, compliance etc.)", 89% said clearly or very clearly. Yet over half of SOE respondents reported that integrity in their SOE is somewhat hampered by "a lack of awareness among employees of the need for, or priority placed on, integrity" (53%). A further almost a half (47%) of SOE respondents also reported "a lack of awareness of legal requirements" as being an obstacle to integrity in the company. Indeed, SOE respondents within the same companies differed in their response as to whether their own integrity-related programmes were established voluntarily or because they were required by the legal framework.

All countries have a certain degree of stratification of related laws, regulations, policies and guidelines that comprise the legal framework. Some state-ownership entities see their expectations as adequately communicated through reading of such laws. Other countries have aimed to provide a degree of centralisation by extracting and highlighting relevant guidelines in one spot, or by taking a stance on the approach SOEs should take.

The ownership entities' expectations and related policies should be consistent with existing requirements, making requirements easily understood by management and boards. Good examples of state-ownership entities centralising and making explicit their expectations with regards to integrity and anti-corruption in SOEs are as follows:

- New Zealand clearly articulates that "Shareholding Ministries expect Crown Company boards to adhere to the 'no surprise policy' and be informed well in advance of everything considered potentially contentious in the public arena, whether the issue is inside or outside the relevant legislation and/or ownership policy." Examples of information that fall within the "no surprise" policy include changes in CEOs, potential or actual conflicts of interest, potential or actual litigation by or against the company or its directors or employees, fraudulent acts, breaches of corporate social responsibility obligations, the release of significant information under the official information act and imminent media coverage of activities that could raise criticism and beg for a response from shareholding ministries (CCMAU, 2007; OECD, 2010).
- Sweden's Ownership Policy: State-owned enterprises should act as role models within the area of sustainable business and should otherwise behave in a manner that promotes public confidence. Exemplary conduct includes working strategically and transparently with a focus on cooperation. These efforts are guided by international guidelines that include provisions on anti-corruption, such as the ten principles of the UN Global Compact and the OECD guidelines for Multinational Enterprises. The ownership policy lays down that it is particularly important that SOEs among other things work towards high standards of business ethics and active prevention of corruption. The ownership policy clarifies that one way of acting as a role model within the areas of anti-corruption and business ethics is to comply with the Code regarding gifts, rewards and other benefits in business established by the Swedish Anti-Corruption Institute.
- Norway's White Paper: Companies are expected to establish guidelines, systems and measures in place to prevent corruption and to address possible or borderline violations that might be detected in this area; and Companies are expected to perform diligent assessments of corruption-related issues in relation to their undertakings. If such assessments point to reasonable doubt as to whether behaviours may be construed as corrupt, the companies are expected to refrain from such behaviours. Norwegian companies that partook in the SOE survey confirm a clear understanding of a zero-tolerance approach to corruption.
- National anti-corruption reforms in Mexico (LGRA) established mechanisms to prevent administrative faults and corruption in the public sector, as well as in SOEs, requiring: an internal control body and supervisory/monitoring body, audit committees, internal audit, external auditor, responsibility units, code of ethics, and a National system of public servants and individuals sanctioned of the National Digital Platform.
- Other countries are engaged in relevant ongoing reforms. For instance, France's APE is working on the development of a shareholder state policy on corporate social and environmental responsibility. This should include a section on integrity and the fight against corruption. Law 2016-1691 requires SOEs to have seven anti-corruption and integrity-related items including a code of conduct, a warning

system and risk mapping process. Iceland is reviewing ownership policy to include provisions on conflict of interest.

Where ownership entities have explicitly included integrity-related mechanisms in their ownership policies or guidelines, there is scope to highlight the linkages between such mechanisms (internal control, risk and audit) with integrity, and their importance for mitigating, as is done in the examples above. Examples where related mechanisms are treated in centralised documents are as follows (OECD, 2016a):

- regarding the related topic of risk management in SOEs, "Iceland,[3] the Philippines,[4] and Poland,[5] have guidance and/or risk management expectations included in the state ownership policy (Iceland) and/or state ownership guidelines or principles (Philippines and Poland)"
- in Switzerland, SOEs' state-decreed strategic objectives include as a standard objective an adequate risk management system in accordance with international risk-management standards, such as ISO 31000 or similar.

In recent years, countries have sought to harmonise laws and regulations, or centralising requirements in one place in attempts to keep pace with the internationalisation of SOEs and demands on their performance (OECD, 2015a; World Bank, 2014). Modernising SOE-related legislation has and continues to provide opportunities for governments to simplify, bring coherence and improve legal requirements of SOEs with respect to integrity, ethics and corporate social responsibility. Recent reforms in Mexico, Colombia and Brazil both in areas of SOE ownership as well as in anti-corruption regulations tackle the issue of corruption more concretely. At the international level, the OECD's 2015 revision of the SOE Guidelines integrated the issue explicitly.

If governments do not communicate and highlight the importance of such laws and regulations, either in writing or in person, there is a risk that the understanding of their importance, and more critically of the requirements and guidance, suffers. This is particularly the case where certain provisions are voluntary.

Thus, governments may wish to consider whether, if at all, the legal and regulatory framework for SOEs can be improved – harmonised or clarified – to promote anti-corruption and integrity in light of the aforementioned challenges to integrity and corruption risks present across OECD member countries and non-member economies. In particular, the state may wish to consider:

- Whether existing requirements promote a level playing field: The legal and regulatory framework for SOEs, regardless of the form it takes, should ensure a level playing field and fair competition in the marketplace – that is, without discriminating between SOEs and market competitors. SOEs undertaking economic activities should not be exempt from the application of general laws, tax codes and regulations (OECD, 2015a: III). In considering the promotion of anti-corruption and integrity, governments should also consider how requirements in anti-corruption and integrity advantage or disadvantage SOEs, seeking to remedy any legal provision that proves it so.
- Whether there is scope to develop an ownership policy or corporate governance code that gives due consideration to anti-corruption and integrity, or to update existing cedes and policies to better emphasise its importance where it does exist.

Communicating clear state expectations on anti-corruption and integrity

The communication of state expectations with respect to, or in addition to, anti-corruption and integrity laws, regulations, and policies impacts the understanding that is fostered and their implementation. Eighty-three percent of SOE respondents said that the state ownership unit/department/agency clearly communicated its expectations for integrity and anti-corruption for their company in the last 12 months, while 17% said it had not.

Those that did not see state expectations as being clearly communicated were more likely to have seen corruption risks in their companies materialise in the last three years (45%, compared to the average of 42%). Recalling that the severity of such corruption risks under assessment varies, all risks included in the assessment represent a vulnerability to the company and its internal controls, risk management and audit processes.

Table 3.2 provides an overview of the participating state ownership entities' approaches to communicating expectations and anti-corruption and integrity provisions. Generally, this is done in reliance on familiarity with existing laws, through supporting documentation (e.g. guidance or memorandums) or through in-person interactions (e.g. annual general meetings, investor, quarterly or ad-hoc meetings, seminars).

Table 3.2. Communicating state expectations on state-owned enterprise integrity and anti-corruption

Country	Ownership Structure	Ownership entity or co-ordination agency	Applied methods for communicating expectations on anti-corruption and integrity		
			Through laws, Regulations and Policies pertaining to SOEs (see Table 4.1)	Through supporting documentation	Through in person interaction: Meetings (M), Trainings and Seminars (T+S),
Argentina	Co-ordinating agency	Chief of the Cabinet of Ministers' Office (JGM)	x	x*	M, T+S
Brazil	Decentralised	Secretariat of Coordination and Governance (SEST)			M
Canada	Hybrid	Crown Corporations Centre of Expertise (COE) in TBS (Priorities and planning sector)	x	x	M, T+S
Chile	Hybrid	Sistema de Empresas (SEP)	x	x	M, T+S
Colombia	Co-ordinating agency	Ministry of Finance		x	
Czech Republic	Dual	Ministry of Finance	x	x	M
Denmark	Hybrid	Ministry of Finance	x		M
Finland	Decentralised	Ownership Steering Department of the Prime Minister's Office of Finland	x		M
France	Centralised	The Government Shareholding Agency (APE: l'Agence des participations de l'État) under the Ministry of Economy			M
Greece	Dual	Ministry of Finance/Privatization & Equity Management Unit	x		

Hungary	Centralised	Hungarian National Asset Management Inc. (HNAM)	x	x	M
Iceland	Centralised	Ministry of Finance and Economic Affairs.	x		
Italy	Dual	Ministry of Economics and Finance, Department of Treasury, institution in charge for SOE shareholder's rights	x	x	
Japan	Decentralised	Split between various ministries	x		
Kazakhstan	Hybrid	Similar to a dual model, split between the Ministry of National Economy, the Committee of State Property and Privatization of the Ministry of Finance, and the authorised body of relevant sector		x**	
Korea	Centralised	Ministry of Strategy and Finance of Korea	x	x	x
Latvia	Co-ordinating agency	Cross-sectoral Coordination Centre			M, T+S
Mexico	Decentralised	Ministry of Finance (SGCP: Secretaría de Hacienda y Crédito Público)	x	x	M
Netherlands	Centralised	MOF	x		
Norway	Centralised (with exceptions)	Ownership Department of Ministry of Trade, Industry and Fisheries - role for coordinating interministerial cooperation on ownership	x	x	x
Paraguay	Centralised	The National Council of Public Enterprises (CNEP)	x	x	
Peru	Centralised	Fondo Nacional de Financiamiento de la Actividad Empresarial del Estado (FONAFE)	x	x	T+S
Philippines	Dual	Governance Commission for Government-Owned or Government Controlled Corporations (GCG)		x	
Poland	Centralised (with exceptions)	Treasury of the Chancellery	x		
Slovenia		Centralised	x		M
Sweden	Centralised	Ministry of Enterprise and Innovation	x		x
Switzerland	Dual	Line Ministries and Federal Finance Administration - FFA	x		M
Turkey	Twin Track model	The Privatisation Administration (PA) is an executive body that directs the restructuring and privatisation process of SOEs.7Most SOEs are still solely under Treasury, Directorate General of State-Owned Enterprises.		x	x
TOTALS		**28**	**21**	**15**	**18**

Note: *Argentina is currently preparing *Guidelines on the Good Governance of SOEs;* ** in Kazakhstan, approving their development strategies and development plans;

Source: OECD 2017 Survey of anti-corruption and integrity in SOEs; more information about ownership structures is found in the forthcoming OECD Compendium on SOE Governance.

Five countries rely alone on the existence of relevant laws to communicate the state's expectations, as shown (Table 3.2). The state ownership entity may place responsibility on the board to ensure their implementation and to communicate appropriately within the SOE about integrity. Many ownership entities do not see further activity as within their role. While the laws may be clear, ownership entities should give due consideration to the understanding of those laws at the board level and within the SOEs, and as to whether or not a more active role for the owner is appropriate and necessary to streamline and harmonise integrity efforts across the country.

Ownership entities should keep in mind that board members are involved in 19% of corruption risks materialising in surveyed companies in the last three years, and that board members have different risk perceptions than others, namely those in integrity-related functions like audit and legal.

Ownership entities may choose to engage further on the topic, considering additional opportunities to communicate expectations if reliance on the board is proving insufficient, drawing inspiration from the following examples:

- ✓ Inclusion of anti-corruption and integrity in **ownership expectations**:
  - New Zealand captures requirements in the Owner's Expectations Manual.
- Inclusion in SOE or board performance objectives:
  - In Colombia, specific objectives are to be set for strategic and majority owned companies by the Ministry of Finance throughout 2018 according to the new strategy for managing the SOE's portfolio that will be released by the end 2017: financial goals; public policy impact; disclosure of information regarding international standards; anticorruption prevention plan.
- Specific **ownership initiatives** on the subject:
  - A Russian SOE reported that the state ownership entity proposes that companies join the anticorruption charter of Russian business and that it sets requirements to create a road map on implementation of anticorruption policies and procedures.
- Awareness raising through exposure to **government-wide anti-corruption initiatives**, such as the development of government-wide AC programmes, audits by the state audit institution, reforms and revision to existing laws or codes:
  - co-ordination in Italy: the Ministry of Economy and Finance and the Italian National Anti-Corruption Authority set up a dedicated working group to define shared guidelines for SOEs partly or totally owned, both at the central and local level.
- Reviewing statements of intent of SOEs with board members, as happens in New Zealand.
- Providing guidance, including sharing good practices and lessons learned:
  - Integrity Consulting in Korea.
  - Sharing good practices as is done in Czech Republic, Denmark, Finland and Latvia.
  - In the United Kingdom the ownership entity established a working group to share best practice both within the departmental group and further afield via guest speakers and presentations by experts in the field of countering fraud, bribery and corruption. Such seminars and external knowledge sharing is also happening in Argentina, having passed their "3rd integrity roundtable" at the time or writing.

  - Brazil's Ministry of Transparency, Supervision and Control has created a Guide for the implementation of the Integrity Program in SOE´s.
- **Written** in letters, circulars, memorandums, and guidelines in support of relevant laws, policies and codes:
  - Colombia's Guide for Directors was designed in order to promote good practices, explain roles and responsibilities, and provide guidance related to the topics that should be covered in a board of directors' session. This guide was delivered to each member of the Board of Directors at the Ministry of Finance. In October 2017, a massive training programme was held for members of the Board of Directors of the Ministry of Finance where topics such as disclosure, transparency and anticorruption were part of the agenda.
- Requiring written confirmation of implementation:
  - In 2017, Colombia required corporate ethics programmes to be put in place. In April 2017 the Superintendence of companies issued a communication to 531 companies, requesting the legal representative to issue a certification stating that such programme was being established.
- **Training** programmes on ethics, anti-corruption and other:
  - Canada: Via the Canadian school of public service, central agencies have developed training for directors and CEOs which includes responsibilities in ethics and integrity; encourages take-up of non-binding standards (not auto applicable to Crown Corporations); advises Crown Corporations that their corporate plans reassure ministers of implementation of ethical practices (e.g. description of risk includes reference to corrupt or unethical behaviour).
  - Chile: the SEP "organises seminars and training programmes for board members and executives of SOEs on a regular basis covering some of the topics tackled in the SEP Guidelines or related corporate governance issues. The efforts are coordinated with the assistance of professional training bodies, such as universities or other public institutions related to the SOEs corporate governance, for example, the General Audit Bureau (Contraloría General de la República), or the financial analysis unit (UAF). Examples of these are the diploma in Corporate Governance for Board members, the workshop on compliance and training for internal audit units undertaken during 2017. The seminars and training programmes that SEP coordinates and provides for board members and executives of its companies frequently includes the participation, as speakers, of members of other public institutions related to the subjects such as internal audit, compliance, risk management, fraud prevention, control and pursuit of corruption, among others."
  - Greece: the ownership entity engages with a more limited scope by providing support and training to all independent internal auditors appointed in non-listed SOEs, about the legal framework and areas of control (i.e. legal compliance, specific areas of control etc.). As mentioned above in Chapter 2, SOEs also have their own training at the SOE level for all staff.
  - Korea: online and off-line education is compulsory in SOEs.
  - Brazil: SEST hosts seminars for all public sector employees including those in state companies. One such seminar was entitled "Good Governance and Strategic Realignment Practices".

Considering the status of state-owned enterprises and their employees vis-à-vis legislation

The majority of companies participating in this study are, given applicable national laws, liable for criminal acts committed by their employees. Almost one-third operate under a strict liability regime, making the company liable as an entity for wrongdoing by all officers, directors/board members, employees or agents acting within their employment and for the benefit of the company. Thirty-eight percent of companies are liable for failure to prevent wrongdoing, but are entitled to a defence of the company to demonstrate that it had adequate compliance or related procedures in place to prevent misconduct. More information about the liability of legal *persons* is found in the OECD's "Liability of Legal Persons for Foreign Bribery: a stock-taking report" (2016d).

When compared to companies with primarily commercial functions, companies in the sample that have a mix of public policy and commercial objectives:

- Are more commonly operating under strict liability regimes, and are less likely to operate under an adjusted liability regime.
- They are more likely than SOEs with entirely commercial objectives to operate under a regime where they are not liable for corruption or other irregular practices;
- Are more likely to have, or have a higher percentage of, representatives considered to be public officials.

The status of an SOE representative as a public official can be a factor when determining which type of legal provisions could apply to a corrupt transaction – and thus for which crime a company may be liable. For instance, bribery of an SOE official in an entirely commercial SOE may be considered "private bribery" (OECD, 2016d). The status of an SOE official may also be a determinant in the applicable liability regime, for instance where the board is a mix of public officials and independents (OECD, 2016d). As a general rule, the status of "public official" within SOEs would be used for:

- Those directly appointed by the state, as a representative of the state, to carry out a public policy objective. This usually refers to the appointment of non-independent board members. Good practice follows that the managerial level should not be appointed to act on behalf of the state. CEOs, for instance, should not be directly appointed by the state.
- Those carrying out a public policy function or objectives daily, whether or not they have been appointed by the state. This is more likely to be seen in SOEs that have a mix of commercial and public policy objectives.

Some SOEs may have "public officials" both at the board and management level. The status may be applied to all (for instance, if an SOE is weakly incorporated), or to individuals based on position. Indeed, multiple respondents within the same company reported having a different status regardless of whether they were a member of the board or executive management.

The presence of public officials - or their differing legal requirements – should not challenge integrity or accountability, yet SOE respondents self-identifying as public officials saw more corruption and other irregular practices in their company in the last three years. They also reported a higher risk of interference in decision-making in their company (43% versus 27%).

The following practices, based on the SOE Guidelines, would help to ensure that the presence of public officials in SOEs is appropriately aligned with the need for execution of policy objectives, and that the associated legal framework does not challenge or confuse accountability or enforcement (2015a):

- Any state representatives nominated to serve on SOE boards should have the equivalent legal responsibilities as other board members.
- Respective personal and state liability should be clarified when state officials are on SOE boards. State officials should have no exemptions from individual responsibility. State officials concerned may have to disclose any personal ownership they have in the SOE and follow the relevant insider trading regulation.
- Guidelines or codes of ethics for members of the ownership entity and other state officials serving as SOE board members could be developed by the ownership entity. They should indicate how information passed on to the state from these board members should be handled.
- Direction in terms of broader policy objectives should be channelled through the ownership entity and expressed as enterprise objectives rather than imposed directly through board participation.
- Persons directly linked with national executive powers should not sit on SOE boards. Other State representatives should be nominated based on qualifications, subject to specific vetting mechanisms;
- Independent board members should be independent from management, government and business relationships. Specific safeguards should be established to verify that nominees comply with requirements.
- SOE boards should be protected from political interference that could prevent them from focusing on achieving the objectives agreed on with the government and the ownership entity. Independence of boards is discussed further in section 3.4.

Promoting good practices and implementation at the enterprise level

An active and informed state sets clear expectations with regards to anti-corruption and integrity, communicates those effectively, and provides indications for their implementation. This sub-section will provide precision on the content on what should be expected from SOEs based on good practices in promoting anti-corruption and integrity at the SOE level (Chapter 2).

Chapters 1 and 2 demonstrated that corruption risks are perceived to be higher where integrity policies and mechanisms, such as audit, are considered to be weak. With this in mind, the state could be more active in encouraging necessary tools in order to support SOEs in meeting other elements of the SOE Guidelines. In addition to the aforementioned and pre-requisite step of setting and communicating clear expectations on the subject, the state can also take other steps to supporting SOEs in effectively preventing corruption and developing a culture of integrity. Good practices in doing so are discussed below.

This report suggests below ways the state can manage the corruption risks presented above, combatting it with a commitment to merit-based and transparent board nomination processes and on-going professional development for board members, robust controls and clear disclosure policies for transparency and reporting.

Contributing to informed, objective and autonomous boards

The board plays a pivotal and central role in SOE governance, acting as an intermediary between the ownership entity and its executive management. A threat to the integrity and professionalism of the board not only threatens the effectiveness of integrity mechanisms in the company, but is a threat to the integrity of the company itself and the boards' decisions meant to be made in the interest of the company.

Aside from the annual shareholders meeting, boards are the top decision-making body of the SOE, yet SOE respondents report a risk of undue influence in decision-making that may include, but not be limited to, undue influence by government officials. They similarly saw a risk of influence in appointments to the board or to the CEO, non-declaration of conflict of interest, and of favouritism, nepotism and cronyism.

The board has a fundamental and ongoing responsibility for the integrity and accountability of the SOE. So too does the state-ownership entity, notably through its role in "establishing well-structured, merit-based and transparent board nomination processes in fully -- or majority-owned SOEs -- actively participating in the nomination of all SOEs' boards and contributing to board diversity" (OECD, 2015a: II.F.2).

The state also has a role in supporting SOE board composition that allows for the exercise of objective and independent judgement. All board members, including any public officials, should be nominated based on qualifications and have equivalent legal responsibilities. For example, in Norway, "ensuring sound composition of boards of companies in which the state is a shareholder is of crucial importance and is one of the Norwegian state's prime responsibilities." Their involvement in so doing involves nominations based on conflict of interest checks, emphasis on competence, capacity and diversity and consideration for corruption risks unique to each company.

This also means establishing a board that is insulated from undue influence. In cases where risk of interference in decision-making is higher, SOE respondents were more likely to have seen corruption risks recently transpire in their company. In cases where interference in appointments is higher, respondents were not more or less likely to have seen corruption. This suggests a need not only to focus efforts only on transparent appointment procedures but on continued application of the merit-based criteria on which they are hired – including high ethical standards – to mitigate undue influence in decision-making of SOEs. Further, the state must also ensure that its interactions with the board, and appointed public officials or representatives on the board, enhance and do not hamper integrity in SOEs. Ensuring integrity in the public sector more broadly is covered further below. Suggested good practices for state ownership entities' contributions to more informed, objective and independent boards are provided below.

Suggested practice for the state: Transparent appointment processes for corporate decision-makers

State ownership entities should establish well-structured, merit-based and transparent board nomination process, in accordance with the SOE Guidelines. States' interpretations of what it means to establish "well-structured, merit-based and transparent board nomination processes" vary. General good practices are provided in Box 3.1. Country practices further below show how countries seek to attract and retain individuals with high ethical standards and professional conduct.

Box 3.1. Good practices in establishing a nomination framework

Nomination frameworks and practice

- A robust nomination framework is one that clearly specifies the nominating power; is transparent; and is consistent in its application.
- Ministerial or Executive powers normally have the ultimate responsibility for nominations. This brings legitimacy to the process, but it should not undermine the role of the ownership function.
- Where feasible, board appointments should be subject to co-ordination or consensus on a whole-of government basis.
- Board appointments, even in wholly-owned SOEs, should be entrusted to the annual general meeting of shareholders.
- Establishing a transparent and consistent method to identify applicants from a wider pool of talent will improve board composition and bring uniformity in the assessment process.
- Specialised bodies in charge of advising or accrediting the nominations can bring further objectivity and transparency to the nomination process.
- The Board should be involved in the nomination process in an advisory capacity.
- Mechanisms should exist to facilitate non-government shareholders participation in the board nomination process.

Source: OECD (2013), *Boards of Directors of State-Owned Enterprises: An Overview of National Practices*, OECD Publishing, Paris. http://dx.doi.org/10.1787/9789264200425-en.

Implementation of the SOE Guidelines should help to mitigate the aforementioned risks of undue influence in decision-making, or influence in appointments. Select country practices for board nominations include:

- In Chile, there is a dedicated working group that undertakes the task of preselecting suitable candidates for the consideration of the council. Similarly, in the Czech Republic there is a committee for the nomination of personnel to which the ownership entity sends its nominations.
- In Colombia, depending on the board, the national government establishes a tentative composition of minimal functional profiles needed by the board as a whole, related to aspects such as knowledge, skills, professional experience, and gender; the government may make use of specialised headhunting firms to provide advice and support to the selection processes. The government's representatives to the boards of directors of its SOEs do not need to be governmental officers necessarily - they may be private sector professionals.
- In Denmark, state officials cannot act as board members or employees of the SOEs. Relevant ministries are required to assess the board composition on a yearly basis in cooperation with the chairman of the board.
- In France, conflict of interest rules are set out on a company-by-company basis, but usually before appointment. When the shareholder directors representing the State are public servants, they are subject to ethics-related obligations which are subject assimilated officials and agents. The state ownership entity keeps a pool of candidates to draw from and includes criteria like age, gender, skills.

To ensure that decisions are made in the best interest of the company, good practice also calls for decisions about executive management to be outside of the jurisdiction for the state. Good practice also calls for the CEO to be separate from the Chair of the Board. Yet, a number of OECD member countries and non-member economies do not fully subscribe to these good practices.

Suggested practice for the state: Furthering the independence and autonomy of boards

SOE respondents in companies with a higher than average proportion of independents on the board, and a lower proportion of political or other state figures, made the following assessments:

- rank the risk of interference in decision-making occurring as lower
- rank the risk of influence in appointments occurring as lower
- rank the risk of favouritism occurring as lower.

A representative of a Supreme Audit Institution (external audit) in Europe reported that the same people who are responsible for supervision within the ministries are nominated to the supervision boards of SOEs, which risks tampering with necessary oversight and accountability.

Limited mandates – in law or in practice – may hinder the autonomy of the board in fulfilling key functions including objective direction and accountability. In cases where the state oversteps or bypasses the board, for instance in appointing a CEO directly, the board's authority and ability to insulate the SOE from undue influence may be challenged.

This finding suggests that state ownership entities should continue with the trend in making boards more independent. It may also wish to give frank consideration to the influence that its own officials are having on SOE boards – whether through their mere presence or through their actions – and the process through which they are appointed (whether directly or indirectly). Above, this chapter discusses the existence of public officials in SOEs. Further below, it discusses how to promote integrity within the public sector more broadly to avoid any potential undue influence in SOEs.

In the survey of 261 SOE representatives, 66% said their companies have requirements for independent board members. Twenty-three percent do not have requirements, and 11% did not know. Definitions of independence and subsequent requirements vary based on country. As mentioned, respondents in companies with a higher number of independent board members rated risks of undue influence as lower.

1. **Independence of boards may be regulated by imposing limitations on the number of years one can serve.** A number of jurisdictions consider that a board member, or director, associated with a company for too many years can no longer be considered independent. The limitations imposed by participating companies ranges from one year to 12 year terms, when "independence" is considered nullified. Reappointments may be made. One Korean company limits the term of the head to three years, while other board members and auditors are limited to 2 years initially, and may be consecutively appointed to one-year terms. In one Latvian company, the limit is 5 years.
2. **Independence may mean both from the company, industry and/or from shareholders.** According to the Finnish Corporate Governance Code, the majority of members must be independent of the company and two members must be

independent of shareholders. A company from the United Kingdom establishes that board members must have no ties to the operating industry.

3. **Independence requirements may differ by the function of each board member.** A company in the Czech Republic has separate independence requirements for members of Audit Committee (by law) and independence of members of Supervisory Board (in practice).

Suggested practice for the state: Clear requirements for conflict of interest at the time of appointment, as well as throughout the duration of members' duties.

Related to the aforementioned requirement for independence, many states establish incompatibilities for board appointments and continuity of their function. The most widely used step for state ownership entities' fulfilment of establishing a transparent and merit-based board is managing conflict of interest, covered in Chapter 1. Ineligibilities reported by the 347 SOE respondents in this study include:

- conflict of interest, or personal interest, with respect to management, government and business relationships
- persons who hold the positions of, or are close to, high level figures in the central directives of political parties or in national directives of trade union or trade union organisations
- persons in teaching positions
- criminal convictions or criminal prosecution for some serious offenses (among these offenses against public service, public trust, property, order Public, public economy, taxation, drug trafficking)
- tax and financial misconduct records, bankruptcy records.

Suggested practice for the state: Including integrity, ethics and the risk profile of the company in the appointment criteria.

State ownership entities may wish to consider how the criteria for nominations and appointments compares in their country, in determining whether a nominee is fit and proper for appointment. In Italy, board members must meet (i) professional requirements, (ii) reputational requirements and (iii) eligibility requirements. A company in Denmark requires yearly declaration of independence from each board member, after the initial appointment. Common practices include:

- proven absence of conflict of interest / state declaration of proper conduct
- integrity, honesty, high morality and/or ethical behaviour
- flawless or impeccable reputation – including passing of security clearances depending on the company
- collaborative, listens carefully, exercises discretion, rational thinker, balanced perspective
- financial competence, and expertise for leadership of special committees (most often audit and risk management)
- justice oriented

Countries apply the above criteria in different ways. In the Netherlands there is a criteria regarding working co-operatively, and in Latvia the ability to create positive relationships. In the United Kingdom, companies reflected their understanding of the principles required of them – the Nolan Principles of Public Life covering (1) selflessness, (2) integrity, (3) objectivity, (4) accountability, (5) openness, (6) honesty, and (7) leadership. Similarly,

Costa Rica has integrity, ethics and objectivity requirements in addition to probity, independence, impartiality and discretion.

Ownership entities may consider introducing criteria for knowledge and understanding of integrity and awareness of corruption risks. While many SOEs include honesty and integrity or risk expertise as part of appointment criteria, not one company reported hiring for anti-corruption expertise. This should be in addition to existing requirements for honesty, given that 40% of SOE respondents report the risk of non-declaration of conflict of interest as a medium or high likelihood of occurrence. Further, the above findings show that specialised board committees – with specialised skills for dealing with integrity and anti-corruption – appear to be effective in reducing the perceived risk of corruption.

Such criteria for anti-corruption and integrity should be reflected in the remuneration policy too. Certain eligibility requirements may be needed, but good practice increasingly relies on tailored approaches to identify the right mix between skills, experience and personal characteristics (OECD, 2013).

Suggested practice for the state: Encouraging the use specialised board committees - at minimum an audit committee

A board or ownership entity may assess the value added of specialised committees, to the extent that one or more are not required in applicable company law. Any assessment of their value should take into account such committees' contributions to preventing corruption and promoting integrity. As shown in prior chapters, respondents in companies with specialised committees report a lower likelihood that corruption risks would materialise in the company.

A financial SOE in the Philippines has established (a) a Board Governance Committee tasked to ensure adherence to principles and standards of good governance to promote transparency and accountability; (b) a Board Audit Committee on compliance with laws, rules and the Code of Ethics; and (c) a Board Risk Management Committee to ensure that the corporation is compliant with the risk management strategy set by the board. Another company in the Philippines has a risk management committee chaired by a representative of the state, or with at least one representative of the state present in the committee.

Suggested practice for the state: Ask SOEs to provide training or induction programmes in which anti-corruption and integrity figure prominently.

Much attention is placed in the SOE Guidelines and other international standards on the process of nominating boards. In view of the above findings, further emphasis should be placed on the presence of mechanisms for continued commitment to transparent, integrity-based activities of members once appointed to the board. For instance, board evaluations can be required and consulted by the state-ownership entity on a more frequent basis.

Trainings could serve as a way to improve effectiveness of board members and to disseminate the importance of anti-corruption and integrity for the achievement of SOE goals. This is in view of the issue that interference in decision-making is a threat that extends past the appointment process. Examples of both types of initiatives are provided in section 3.2.2 as part of an effective communication of states' expectations on anti-corruption and integrity. Board members should be informed that such expectations established in their appointment are to be maintained. For listed companies in Italy, for instance, directors appointed as independent members must immediately inform the board of directors if they no longer meet any of the requirements indicated, as well as of the occurrence of any causes for ineligibility or incompatibility.

Encouraging robust internal controls, risk management, internal and external audit, and ethics and compliance programmes or measures

Effective internal controls are instrumental in the achievement of an SOE's broad mandates and objectives (OECD, 2015a: II.F.3). Boards of SOEs should be responsible for overseeing the development and implementation of internal control activities, including those that contribute to preventing fraud and corruption. These activities should conform to national and international standards and commitments and apply to the SOE and its subsidiaries (OECD, 2015, VC). SOEs should be subject to the same accounting, disclosure, compliance and auditing standards as listed companies.

Thirty-nine percent of SOE survey respondents reported that ineffective internal control or risk management poses an obstacle to integrity in their company. Companies with commercial objectives and companies with public policy objectives equally ranked this as a challenge.

In seeking to adhere to the SOE Guidelines, state ownership entities should continue to promote the strengthening of internal control activities, risk management and audit functions. To the extent that the requirements for internal control are not up to date with the risks and controls explained above in Chapter 2, the ownership entity should review and revisit internal control requirements.

State ownership entities should have adequate measures in place to ensure that SOE boards will oversee the creation and maintenance of an effective internal control system.

Suggested practice for the state: Promoting appropriate internal controls and staying informed about their effectiveness

Practices vary across OECD countries depending on the SOEs' degree of corporatisation and their legal or functional independence from the government. Internal control practices can be divided into three broad categories depending on the degree of an SOEs' functional independence, shown in Figure 3.2 (OECD, 2016).

Regardless of the functional independence of the SOE from the ownership entity, internal control principles can be streamlined across SOEs to ensure consistency in approach within one country. The same can be said for risk management principles. A 2016 OECD study found that risk management systems are only required in about half of 32 surveyed countries in 2016. Less than half were required to establish specialised board committees to oversee risk management (OECD, 2016a).

As part of its monitoring, the state ownership entity could stay abreast of external commentary on the adequacy of internal controls across the portfolio, allowing it to identify gaps or weaknesses in particular SOEs. It is one way in which it can stay more informed.

One third of SOE respondents see ineffective internal control and risk management as a problem for their companies' integrity. As described in Chapter 2, risk management approaches vary by company.

Figure 3.2. Spectrum of internal control models depending on state-owned enterprises' functional independence

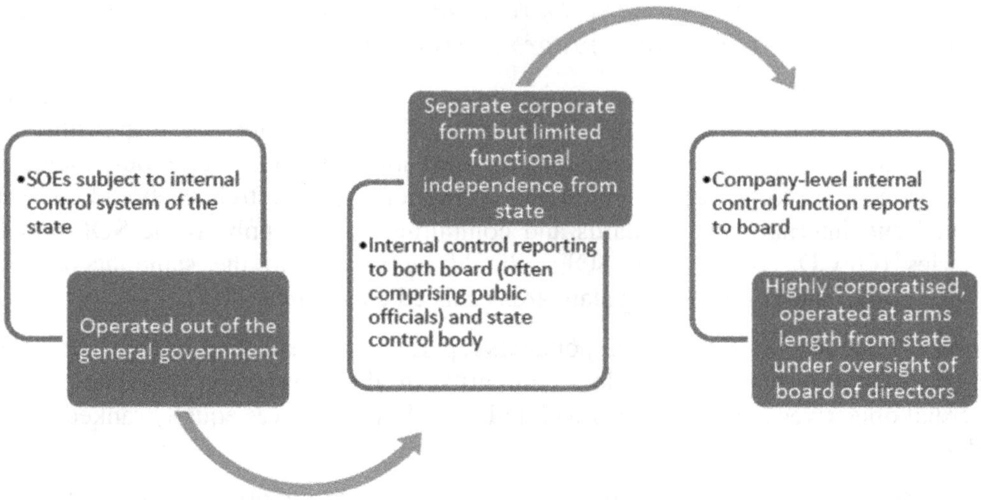

Source: OECD (2016d), Combatting corruption and promoting business integrity in state-owned enterprises: Issues and trends in national practices, Global Knowledge Sharing Network on Corporate Governance of State-Owned Enterprises, 7-8 June, 2016, www.oecd.org/daf/ca/2016-SOEs-issues-paper-anti%20corruption-and-business-integrity.pdf.

Boards are not always duly informed of risks and, in addition, have different risk perceptions than those responsible for designing and implementing appropriate controls. State ownership entities should encourage more robust risk management processes that incorporate corruption risks, and focus on particular risk areas as needed – ensuring requirements are coherent and clear (e.g. procurement). The state could encourage more frequent and regular reporting of risks to the board, or encourage the board to be more active in staying informed.

- Companies in Korea, Poland, Latvia, and Mexico reported that their state ownership entities directly support them in identifying corruption risks;
- Russian companies reported that the state recommends they run a specific anti-corruption risk assessment.

Suggested practice for the state: Requiring regular assessments of corruption risks, as well as their explicit treatment in risk management systems.

Not all SOEs' risk assessments explicitly cover corruption risks. Those companies that do, run such assessments predominantly on an annual basis or every two to three years. The findings show that companies that ran risk assessments of corruption risks every two to three years were more likely to see corruption than those that do so on an annual basis.

Germany's *Federal Government Directive Concerning the Prevention of Corruption in the Federal Administration*, applicable to SOEs, requires identification and analysis of areas of activity especially vulnerable to corruption. The Directive continues in requiring "in all federal agencies, measures to identify areas of activity which are especially vulnerable to corruption shall be carried out at regular intervals and as warranted by circumstances. The use of risk analyses shall be considered for this purpose. The results of the risk analysis shall be used to determine any changes in organization, procedures or personnel assignments" (Federal Ministry of the Interior).

Suggested practice for the state: Encourage improved internal audit and ensuring adequate external audit.

The approaches to internal audit, and the perception of their effectiveness, vary across and within companies. The autonomy, capacity and effectiveness of internal audit are fundamental given its de facto roles and real responsibilities assigned to it across SOEs. International studies also point to the heavy reliance on internal audit for prevention and detection of corruption and irregular practices. The ineffectiveness of external audit is less troublesome for SOEs than ineffectiveness of internal audit or controls. State approaches in this regard could be inspired by Colombia's efforts to strengthen internal and external audit of SOEs (Box 3.2).

Box 3.2. Mechanisms for improving internal and external audit in Colombia

In Colombia, some SOEs have also adopted voluntary policies of rotating their (external) auditors and the directorate for SOEs has pushed to change external auditors at least every four years. SOEs are, in addition, subject to the individual and sector specific supervision of bodies such as the Financial Superintendence, the Utilities Superintendence, the Comptroller General's Office and the General Accounting Office, which also, in one way or another, audit their results. Colombian companies are legally required to have their annual financial statements audited by an external auditor "revisor fiscal". The external or statutory auditor, who is assigned by the general meeting of shareholders may perform this function for no more than five companies at a time. If a public accounting firm is appointed as "revisor fiscal", a partner from the firm or an employee who is legally qualified to practice accounting is designated to perform those duties for no more than four straights years and every two years the designated partner must be changed. A number of additional legal requirements have been established in support of auditor independence. The external auditor cannot provide non-audit services for the company he or she audits, and in case of violation, may be sanctioned by the Central Board of Accountants. In addition, according to the Commercial Code, the statutory auditor may not be 1) a partner of the company or any of its subsidiaries or those associated with or employees of the parent; 2) linked by marriage or relationship or are co-members of board members or managers, the auditor cashier or company itself; or 3) employed by the company or its subordinate.

Source: Material provided by the Co-ordinating Agency in Colombia's Ministry of Finance.

State ownership entities may wish to encourage greater uptake of performance audits – whether internal or external, while avoiding unnecessary duplication. Performance audits give a more well-rounded view of the entity in question.

Section 2.2.7 outlines the various ways in which state auditors, or Supreme Audit Institutions, can play a complementary role in assessing the effectiveness of individual SOEs, groups of SOEs and the governance arrangements between SOEs and the state and within the SOE itself.

Developing a disclosure policy and encouraging reporting and transparency

In order to ensure adequate accountability by SOEs to shareholders, reporting bodies and the broader public, the state as an owner should develop "a disclosure policy for SOEs that identifies what information should be publicly disclosed, the appropriate channels for disclosure, and mechanisms for ensuring quality of information" (SOE Guideline II.F.5). They should face disclosure requirements for listed companies, giving regard to the capacity and size of the SOE (OECD, 2015a).

For SOEs that combine economic activities and public policy objectives, high standards of transparency and disclosure regarding their cost and revenue structures must be maintained, allowing for an attribution to main activity areas. For SOEs that are partially owned by the state, such disclosure should also be provided to all other shareholders. Due regard should be made for the size and capacity of the enterprise in requiring certain information – with larger, listed enterprises usually required to disclose more than small and medium-sized SOEs. Development of a disclosure policy should:

- Be based on a review of gaps and involve structured consultations with SOE boards and management, as well as with regulators, members of the legislature and other relevant stakeholders.
- Be based, to the extent possible, on a cost-benefit analysis to determine which SOEs should be submitted to high quality internationally recognised standards. This analysis should consider that demanding disclosure requirements are both an incentive and a means for the board and management to perform their duties professionally.
- Requiring disclosure of remuneration of board members and key executives on an individual basis (such as termination and retirement provisions, specific benefits or in-kind remuneration to board members).

The policy should be communicated widely, which can be done through the development of guidance manuals and training seminars for SOEs; special initiatives such as performance awards that recognise individual SOEs for high quality disclosure practices; and mechanisms to measure, assess and report on implementation of disclosure requirements by SOEs. Good practice calls for the use of web-based communications to facilitate access by the general public. This is also a channel through which state ownership entities can stay and fulfil tasks of monitoring (discussed below) and reporting annually on SOEs.

SOEs should report material financial and non-financial information on the enterprise in line with high quality internationally recognised standards of corporate disclosure, and including areas of significant concern for the state as an owner and the general public. This includes in particular SOE activities that are carried out in the public interest. A Norwegian SOE gave accolades to the state ownership entity for opening up a transparent 'reporting culture' between company and state when there might be issues at hand.

Examples of the types of information that an ownership entity may include in the disclosure policy, and thus require from SOEs, appear in Table 3.3. SOEs in the sample are consistent in reporting financial and operating results, statements of objectives and their fulfilment, and information on the governance and ownership of the enterprise.

Two in five publicly disclose "any financial assistance, including guarantees, received from the state and commitments made on behalf of the SOE, including contractual commitments and liabilities arising from public-private partnerships". This is despite the fact that a high-level of disclosure should be required for SOEs, notably with respect to any subsidies or preferential treatment, and particularly for those pursuing public policy objectives. Yet SOEs with entirely commercial objectives report to disclose financial assistance slightly more often that SOEs with policy objectives, suggesting a greater need for transparency in the ownership and financial assistance to SOEs pursuing policy objectives. Only one third report on material risk factors.

Table 3.3. The extent of state-owned enterprise disclosure

	Information to be disclosed	% of respondents whose companies disclose:
1.	A clear statement to the public of enterprise objectives and their fulfilment (for fully-owned SOEs this would include any mandate elaborated by the state ownership entity);	78%
2.	Enterprise financial and operating results, including where relevant the costs and funding arrangements pertaining to public policy objectives;	96%
3.	The governance, ownership and voting structure of the enterprise, including the content of any corporate governance code or policy and implementation processes;	81%
4.	The remuneration of board members and key executives;	72%
5.	Board member qualifications, selection process, including board diversity policies, roles on other company boards and whether they are considered as independent by the SOE board;	52%
6.	Any material foreseeable risk factors and measures taken to manage such risks;	34%
7.	Any financial assistance, including guarantees, received from the state and commitments made on behalf of the SOE, including contractual commitments and liabilities arising from public-private partnerships;	40%
8.	Any material transactions with the state and other related entities.	43%

Note: The elements for disclosure are taken from the SOE Guidelines as examples of what could be disclosed, with consideration for the size and capacity of the SOE.
Source: OECD 2017 Survey of anti-corruption and integrity in SOEs.

Suggested practice for the state: Consider expanding the disclosure policy or enhancing requirements regarding corruption-related risks.

A low proportion of respondents' companies report any foreseeable material risk factors and measures taken to manage such risks. Given the previously identified need to strengthen the inclusivity of risk assessments and the fact that some companies do not treat corruption risks separately, consistent reporting of material risks may allow for early warning and red flag detection.

State ownership entities could assess whether disclosure requirements should be expanded or altered based on SOEs' current disclosures in comparison to list above (Table 3.3). Any modifications to disclosure policies should give due consideration to the potential for any advantages or disadvantages to SOEs compared to private firms, and should be made in consultation with the boards.

Some companies go further yet in their disclosure and set a good example of transparent entities that can help to build client and public trust. Inspired by those enterprises that put efforts into transparency and reporting, state ownership entities could promote more proactive disclosure with elements that provide insight into the efficacy of integrity functions. Based on real company examples, this could include:

- any procurement bids, procurement plans or contracts
- internal Audit reports
- final manager reports when leaving the position
- requests made under an Access to Information Act
- performance scorecards
- major litigations.

Monitoring integrity in state-owned enterprises as part of performance monitoring

A primary responsibility of the state in good corporate governance is "setting up reporting systems that allow the ownership entity to regularly monitor, audit and assess SOE performance, and oversee and monitor their compliance with applicable corporate governance standards" (OECD, 2015a: II.F.4).

Disclosure and reporting by SOEs, as discussed above, can help to facilitate continuous oversight. It is in the state's interest to ensure such disclosure and reporting systems are adequate to render high-quality and accurate information on SOE performance. The existence of effective monitoring by the state supports greater transparency and accountability of SOEs. It communicates to SOEs that misconduct will not go unnoticed.

Performance monitoring becomes doubly beneficial for performance, accountability and transparency when assessments explicitly include commentary on the sufficiency of SOE approaches to integrity and anti-corruption.

The reporting systems should give the ownership entity a true picture of the SOE's performance and financial situation, enabling it to react on time and to be selective in its intervention. An audit of state ownership of SOEs by a European state audit institution concluded that the state does not have sufficient information on risks. If the board relies on management to determine what material is and should be reported, where they have differing views, then the state also relies on a chain of reporting as to what is material. The ownership policy and disclosure policy should clarify that risks should be reported and include corruption related risks. The state should encourage boards to be active and require/request from management the relevant information.

Suggested practice for the state: Integrating SOEs' integrity and anti-corruption efforts into regular performance monitoring.

Not all state ownership entities consider anti-corruption and integrity as part of performance. Being well informed about SOE performance should be synonymous with understanding its performance and the effectiveness, efficiency and economy of internal controls, such as audit, and risk management, instrumental in facilitating the achievement of objectives set by the state. These can also be critical for mitigating corruption that can detract from goal achievement. Ownership entities can integrate anti-corruption and integrity into the main steps of effective, ongoing monitoring (OECD, 2010):

- regular information on performance by SOE boards
- systematic information processes put in place

- develop specific "continuous information"' and/or "no surprise" policy
- complementary information channels
- use of external information available
- performance check-up by the ownership entity
- regular (quarterly) meetings between boards and ownership entities
- feedback by the ownership entity on current performance
- revision of targets
- ad hoc meetings
- in case of serious underperformance, take action.

In the UK, a quarterly "Traffic Light" review is done for each SOE. This review evaluates the quality of the shareholder relationship, the implementation of the shareholder model, the quality of the board and management team, the strategy and financial performance. For each of these categories, a series of questions are to be answered by "yes" or "no" by the portfolio manager with a possibility to comment also. All, or nearly all, "yes" answers give an overall green light, some specific "no" answers may trigger a red light, otherwise the light is amber. (This type of "traffic light" review is sometimes criticised for lacking nuance.) For each category, in addition to the general appreciation, the portfolio manager must indicate the action taken to improve the situation. An aggregate monitoring table is then built up, indicating for each SOE the colour of the light for each of the categories mentioned above. This is a type of control board for the executive shareholders work (OECD, 2010).

A specific and interesting process is being developed in Greece in the framework of the current broad reforms of SOE governance. A specific management information system has been put in place to collect the relevant data directly from the SOEs' own information systems to monitor their performance. This will constitute a unique system to monitor closely and frequently an SOEs' performance. Monthly data will be automatically compared to budget data. The whole system of business plans, budget and performance monitoring will be based on the same data, allowing a closer monitoring and thus greater transparency and accountability (OECD, 2010).

The Slovenian Sovereign Holding, one of three state owners, can request SOEs to submit special reports on integrity or anti-corruption and may discuss them in regular meetings with the management of SOEs. SOEs with over 500 employees during the fiscal year are required to report in annual business reports on environmental, social and human resources matters, as well as respect for human rights and the fight against corruption and bribery.

The state could enlist systematic benchmarking of SOE performance, with private or public sector entities, both domestically and abroad. For SOEs with no comparable entity against which to benchmark overall performance, comparisons can be made concerning certain elements of their operations and performance. Benchmarking should cover productivity and the efficient use of labour, assets and capital. This benchmarking is particularly important for SOEs operating in sectors where they do not face competition. It allows the SOEs, the ownership entity and the general public to better assess SOE performance and reflect on their development (OECD, 2015a).

As mentioned above, state ownership entities share good practices, as well as lessons learned. The ownership entity of Norway now undertakes "best practice" studies, encouraging companies to share experiences and best practices. Other countries may use an integrity "track record" or white list to provide positive recognition for efforts. In fewer cases, states share "bad practices" of other SOEs or public entities. Consideration can be given as to whether or not to make such information public. In New Zealand, the state ownership entity publicly exposes any practices which fall short of these standards.

Some states have sanctioned studies by independent third parties to bolster their understanding of SOEs or of key issues they face (as is done in Sweden and Norway). Others systematically mandate and review board evaluations and external audit reports. In Finland, annual board evaluations are required with the methodology at the discretion of the SOE, ranging from hiring a third party/consultant or the board conducting surveys of the SOE. In Sweden, a sustainability analysis tool is used, with sustainability reporting equipped with teams to review (Box 3.3).

Box 3.3. State-ownership methodologies for assessing state-owned enterprise performance with regards to integrity and the fight against corruption

Sustainability analysis tool in Sweden

A sustainability analysis tool that sheds light on relevant areas of sustainable business, including corruption and business ethics, has been developed for state-owned companies by the Government Offices corporate management organisation. The analysis increases the owner's awareness of the companies' risks and opportunities and how these are managed. This includes a review of the sector, country and company sustainability-related risks linked to the value chain and the corporate governance framework for these aspects. The result of the analysis is communicated to the board of the company. It is also integrated in corporate governance and taken into account in the Government's regular dialogue with the company in monitoring the company's development, and in the recruitment and nomination of board members.

Source: Materials provided by the Swedish division for SOEs under the Ministry of Enterprise and Innovation.

Many ownership entities are in the habit of using external audits – whether state or non-state. Ownership entities may do this to stay informed. Latvia uses reports of the Supreme Audit Institution to consult on SOE matters including any identified deficiencies in governance at national and municipal levels. In the Czech Republic and Greece the ownership entities rely on internal and external audits for monitoring.

Ownership entities may do this to hold SOEs to account, where the owner reviews and follows-up with the SOE as needed. In the Philippines, the SAI sends the ownership entity its audits periodically to support its monitoring and the take-up of audit findings. Iceland too follows up on red flags raised in audit reports.

Responding to cases of corruption and other irregular practices in state-owned enterprises

An underexplored area regarding the state's role in ownership of enterprises is in their responsibilities and response in cases of suspected, and proven, corruption-related misconduct. Similarly important is that SOEs also have appropriate and measured recourse in cases of potential irregular practices that may be linked to corrupt activities or have weakened the entity to such activities.

Indeed, many states seem to be applying piecemeal approaches to managing potential and real corruption, ranging from the ownership entity leaving involvement completely to other relevant state authorities (prosecutors, auditors and other law enforcement) to following each step of the process beginning with red flags of potential misconduct. Often, the degree of state-ownership entities' involvement is determined on a case-by-case basis. Most ownership entities are simply informed and let boards manage it, while others require evidence of what went wrong.

All state ownership entities in the survey reported that the SOEs have an obligation to inform a relevant public entity of potential infraction – with different thresholds for the severity warranting flagging. They are usually required to inform their oversight ministry, as n Latvia, where the responsible line ministry could suspend those involved, or require internal investigation or external audit.

Instead, some ownership entities take an "observer role". Leaving it to the responsibilities of other competent authorities is not inherently problematic. However, without adequate follow-up or an effort to understand what went wrong, it becomes a lost opportunity for the ownership entity to understand where weaknesses in their portfolios exist and where others may be able to learn.

The state's involvement may depend on the legal status of SOE employees, and the liability of the firm. In France, there are no specific actions undertaken by the APE, but if the issue is raised by the board then a more in-depth discussion with relevant committees would occur. Normally, according to Article 17 of the *Loi Sapin*, responsibility is handed over to the French Anti-Corruption Agency: "Irrespective of the liability of the natural persons referred to in Article 17 (I), the company shall also be liable as a legal person in the event of failure to fulfil the above obligations. Monitoring compliance with these obligations, which define a general obligation to prevent corruption, falls within the competence of the French Anti-Corruption Agency (AFA)".

While responsibility may be shared between different state authorities, the approach in cases of suspected misconduct should not be treated as an afterthought. SOEs and state ownership entities may benefit from a clear plan of action and understanding of who is to be involved and when.

Consideration should be given to the complexity and burden of regulations that are in place to, in theory, mitigate offenses that do occur. Overly burdensome regulations or controls can have negative effects. A 2015 study from PwC and the London School of Business "on promoting ethical behaviour in the financial services sector shows that a "gettough" approach to the management of performance has created a climate of fear which, in turn, leads to unethical behaviours. The study found that anxiety caused by this blame culture disrupts people's capacity to make good decisions – and often leads them to behave less well than those who are motivated by the potential positive outcomes of success" (PwC, 2015).

Some hold the belief that negating rules, and engaging in corruption can, in fact, promote economic growth. An OECD Issues Paper for the G20 on the Impact of Corruption on Economic Growth (2014), tackles such an allegation, finding that choosing to remove and clarify regulations can have a more positive effect on GDP growth than circumventing rules through corruption where existing rules are growth-impeding. Further, an explicit and transparent industrial policy should achieve results that are equal or superior to close ties or cronyism between public officials and industry leaders.

Governments may, in certain cases, have incentive to disregard potential misconduct in or around an SOE, given the potential repercussions it may have for public trust in SOEs, or in government. This may be a particularly relevant concern where the state is considering reputational damage in a context where SOEs are more active abroad and represent a larger share of government GDP. This should not be a deterrent from the state enforcing appropriate action. Other relevant investigative and enforcement authorities must be involved, whether directed by the board or by the ownership entity.

Suggested practice for the state: Develop transparent procedures for handling suspected and real cases of suspected corruption in accordance with the severity of the potential misconduct and the position of those involved.

Given the loss of trust in government, governments may be incentivised to make the requirement for SOEs to duly inform the ownership entity systematic. Breaches may happen in the daily operations of the companies whose autonomy ownership entities are trying to respect. While the state ownership entity cannot predict, they can require disclosure about corruption risks (as discussed above) and request to be informed when a breach happens. Where the state is not a majority shareholder, other shareholders should be duly informed.

Internal and external investigation immediately with results being shared with the ownership entity and as needed to other major shareholders who decide how to proceed.

- In Finland, investigations are initiated without delay both externally and internally. Also a special auditing is carried out by an external auditor. A professional legal aid can also be used. The findings and conclusions are reported immediately thereafter to the state ownership entity (and, as the case may be, to other major shareholders), who decides how to proceed in the matter. The minister responsible for steering the ownership is also informed. Person(s) who are under investigation are removed from his/hers/their position(s) in the company. If the investigations indicate any corruption or other irregular practices, the case will be moved to the police for investigation and, as the case may be, later to the public prosecutor (district attorney). The prosecutor decides, whether to take the case to the court or not. The company and the state ownership entity (and, as the case may be, the other major shareholder[s]) mutually decide when, if ever, and how to publish the case.
- Canada's ownership is a hybrid model of decentralised and co-ordinated ownership, with responsible ministers in charge of specific Crown Corporations (at the Federal level), and other central agencies co-ordinating across Crown Corporations. Any infraction involving top management would be generally dealt with at the SOE level, while issues at the board level would be dealt with by the government through the channel with appropriate jurisdiction over the subject matter of the reported behaviour (e.g., financial mismanagement would engage the Auditor General or potentially external auditors; conflicts of interest/ethics would engage the responsible Commissioner; or actions may come out through whistleblower action through the Integrity Commissioner). Where there is sufficient ground to investigate the matter as criminal behaviour, the appropriate law enforcement body would be engaged. The minister responsible would be answerable to Parliament with respect to actions taken.

Consistent plans will importantly help to reduce the concern that SOEs are protected or exempt from enforcement – demonstrating that there are specific steps and actors assigned, that can be tracked.

Suggested practice for the state: Conducting follow up, demanding proof of remedy, and sharing lessons-learned.

At a minimum, the state should be informed about any corruption cases, regardless of the extent of its involvement in any investigative process in order to consider the need for improvements in its own approach, or that of the SOE.

Countries could go beyond the minimum of staying informed, by sharing lessons learned as does the ownership entity of Denmark, according to one SOE respondent. In Norway, the ownership entity follows-up with the board to discuss what happened and to prevent future infractions.

Following integrity concerns in a Dutch company, the relevant Ministry requested several investigations and has since monitored and followed-up on the results. Furthermore, the Minister appointed an executive director in the area of Risk and Compliance. Such appointments in response to allegations of corruption or other rule breaking should, as in any appointment by the state, be considered in consultation with the board and be made with transparency and in considering merit and incompatibility.

The natural reaction should not be to compromise the autonomy and independence of the board. The state should continue to limit its instructions to the board to strategic issues, leaving decision-making to the board. However, the state-ownership entity may use such opportunities to revisit its annual performance monitoring processes to determine whether or not the state was adequately informed of the risks. Box 3.4 outlines the approaches that Brazil's SEST has taken (Statute of SOEs and of Decree 8,945/2016) to deter future corruption and integrity breaches in SOEs.

Box 3.4. Implementing state-owned enterprise reform: Brazil's 2016 Statute of State-Owned Enterprises

In June 2016, the Brazilian Congress passed Law 13.303/2016 known as the Statute of SOEs. The first section of the Law is dedicated to establishing a corporate governance framework for SOEs, while the second establishes a new set of rules for the procurement processes of those companies. Key requirements of the Statute of SOEs includes:

- All SOEs must draft and publish an annual letter subscribed to by the members of the board of directors, publicising its public policy objectives, and the ones of its subsidiaries, in line with the collective interest or imperative of national security that justified its creation. The letter must contain a clear definition of the resources to be applied for such a purpose, as well as the economic and financial impacts of meeting such objectives, which must be measurable by means of objective indicators.
- All SOEs must establish an integrity department, headed by an Executive Director, directly reporting to the CEO. The Law also states that, in the event of the CEO's involvement with a suspected irregularity or if the CEO fails to take action towards a specific case, the integrity officer must be able to report directly to the board of directors.
- All SOEs must provide to all personnel, at least once a year, training on the Code of Conduct and integrity policies, including high-level administration.

- All the executive directors and members of the Board must be trained, when they are appointed and at least once a year thereafter. The contents of the trainings should be related to internal controls, the code of conduct, anticorruption law, information disclosure, capital markets and corporate law. The Statute of SOEs also determines that executive directors or board members that do not participate in at least one such training session in a period of two years will not have their mandate renewed by the SOE.
- The Law establishes criteria for the selection, appointment, and evaluation of board members and executive directors that have an unsoiled reputation and reputable knowledge. The criteria for appointment include requisites of professional experience and academic qualifications.
- The Law also prohibits the appointment of those who fall into any of the following criteria, among others: occupants of political positons (such as ministers and secretaries of state, municipal secretaries); representatives of regulatory bodies to which the SOE is subject; holders of a position without a permanent relationship with the civil service; people who participated in the decision structure of a political party or organisation of an electoral campaign in the last 36 months; and other prohibitions aiming at preventing conflicts of interest or the undue utilisation of the high-rankjng positions in SOEs.
- Each SOE must establish a Committee of Eligibility. This committee is mandated to issue a formal opinion on the compliance of appointments for management positions, members of the boards and fiscal counsel with regards to the requirements and prohibitions contained in the law concerning these nominations.
- The Statute of SOEs determined that SOEs that hold less than 50% of the shares in other companies must develop a "shareholder corporate governance policy" that stipulates governance and control practices proportional to the relevance, materiality and risks of the business. This corporate governance policy must determine, among other things, that the company that has the SOE as its shareholder draft:
    - A report on the risks associated to its construction contracts as well as to contracts for the supply of goods and services relevant to the interests of the investing SOE;
    - A report on the implementation of the policy on related party transactions;
    - A report on the execution of the capital budget and the execution of investments programmed by the company, including information on the alignment between the estimated/realized costs and the market prices.

Note: Information provided by Brazil's Secretariat of Coordination and Governance of SOEs (SEST) within the Ministry of Planning, and the Ministry of Transparency and Office of the Comptroller General – CGU (2017).

Building on the OECD Guidelines for Corporate Governance of State-Owned Enterprises

The above findings demonstrate a wide range of activities, based on real ownership practices, that other ownership entities can use to promote integrity in and around SOEs, keeping in mind the SOE Guidelines' call for a strict separation of roles between the owner and the management of the SOE (the state avoiding hands-on intervention in individual SOEs), and the principle of clear distinction between the state's role as an owner and its other roles (such as supervisory authority, regulator and public prosecutor). They are categorised in broad terms and could act as a basis for future guidance for the state as SOE owners on the topic of integrity and anti-corruption. Based on the good practices of and discussions with participating states, priority areas for states could include:

1. Applying high standards of integrity to those exercising ownership of state-owned enterprises on behalf of the general public.
2. Establishing ownership arrangements that are conducive to integrity.
3. Ensuring clarity in the legal and regulatory framework and in the state's expectations.
4. Acting as an informed and active owner with regards to integrity in SOEs.
5. Requiring adequate risk management systems within SOEs.
6. Requiring adoption of high quality integrity mechanisms within SOEs.
7. Safeguarding the autonomy of SOEs and their decision-making bodies.
8. Requiring objective external review of state-owned enterprises and the ownership function.
9. Taking action and respect due process for investigations and prosecutions.
10. Inviting the inputs of civil society, the public and the press.

Notes

[1] The level or corporatisation is dependent on how integrated the SOE activity is to the public entity to which it is linked, how countries define commercial activities, how a country demarcates its boundaries, and the consideration as to where efficiency gains can be made for government and the marketplace. A higher level of state activity in the marketplace does not, in its own right, represent a threat to competitive neutrality. Scandinavian countries have tended to be successful in securing this, enabling intermingling between both private and public interests within sectors. (OECD, 2012, Comp Neutrality; World Bank, 2014).

[2] This survey refers to the Working Party Risk Management Survey conducted in 2016, results for which are presented in OECD's 2016, Risk Management by State-Owned Enterprises and their Ownership. Countries involved included Argentina, Austria, Belgium, Brazil, Chile, Czech Republic, Denmark, Finland, France, Germany, Greece, Iceland, Ireland, Israel, Italy, Japan, Kazakhstan, Latvia, Lithuania, Mexico, Netherlands, New Zealand, Norway, Poland, Philippines, the People's Republic of China, Portugal, Slovenia, Spain, Sweden, Switzerland, Turkey and the United Kingdom.

[3] Risk management by SOEs is addressed in the Government's 2012 general government ownership policy. Risk management codes are also outlined in the Government's 2009 policy for state-owned financial institutions, which requires the establishment of risk committees that report direct to the board of directors.

[4] The GOCC Governance Act of 2011 provides the general policy framework for the risk management regime within the Philippine SOE sector.

[5] Polish SOEs are expected to comply with the State Treasury's "Principles of Corporate Supervision over Companies with State Treasury Shareholding", newly signed on 28 September 2017, as well as, Guidelines for companies with the State Treasury participation preparing financial statements for 2017 (http://bip.kprm.gov.pl/kpr/bip-kancelarii-prezesa/podmioty-nadzorowane-pr/nadzor-wlascicielski/4320,Nadzor-wlascicielski.html).

References

New Zealand (2012), Owners Expectations Manual, Treasury of New Zealand, https://treasury.govt.nz/publications/guide/owners-expectations-manual-html.

OECD (2017a), OECD Recommendation of the Council on Public Integrity, www.oecd.org/gov/ethics/recommendation-public-integrity/.

OECD (2017b), *The Size and Sectoral Distribution of State-Owned Enterprises*, OECD Publishing, Paris, http://dx.doi.org/10.1787/9789264280663-en.

OECD (2016a), *Risk Management by State-Owned Enterprises and their Ownership*, OECD Publishing, Paris. http://dx.doi.org/10.1787/9789264262249-en.

OECD (2016b), "The ownership and governance of state-owned enterprises", in *State-Owned Enterprises as Global Competitors: A Challenge or an Opportunity?*, OECD Publishing, Paris. http://dx.doi.org/10.1787/9789264262096-9-en

OECD (2016c), Liability of Legal Persons for Foreign Bribery: A Stocktaking Report, www.oecd.org/corruption/liability-of-legal-persons-for-foreign-bribery-stocktaking-report.htm

OECD (2016c), Ethics and Business Integrity in Southern Africa: a handbook for governments as owners and state-owned enterprises, OECD, unpublished, www.oecd.org/daf/ca/soe-africa.htm.

OECD (2016d), Combating corruption and promoting business integrity in state-owned enterprises: Issues and trends in national practices, Global Knowledge Sharing Network on Corporate Governance of State-Owned Enterprises, 7-8 June, 2016, www.oecd.org/daf/ca/2016-SOEs-issues-paper-anti%20corruption-and-business-integrity.pdf.

OECD (2015a), *OECD Guidelines on Corporate Governance of State-Owned Enterprises, 2015 Edition*, OECD Publishing, Paris, www.oecd.org/corporate/guidelines-corporate-governance-soes.htm.

OECD (2015b), Corporate Governance and Business Integrity: A stocktaking of Corporate Practices, OECD Publishing, Paris, www.oecd.org/corruption/corporate-governance-business-integrity-stocktaking-corporate-practices.htm.

OECD (2014), Issues paper for G20 on corruption and economic growth, www.oecd.org/g20/topics/anti-corruption/Issue-Paper-Corruption-and-Economic-Growth.pdf

OECD (2013), *Boards of Directors of State-Owned Enterprises: An Overview of National Practices*, OECD Publishing, Paris, http://dx.doi.org/10.1787/9789264200425-en

OECD (2010), *Accountability and Transparency: A Guide for State Ownership*, OECD Publishing, Paris, http://dx.doi.org/10.1787/9789264056640-en

World Bank, Corporate Governance of State-Owned Enterprises A Toolkit, Chapter 2: Legal and Regulatory Framework, World Bank, Washington DC, https://openknowledge.worldbank.org/bitstream/handle/10986/20390/9781464802225.pdf

Annex A. Respondent characteristics

Table A A.1. Number of respondents by country

Participating country	State ownership questionnaire	SOE survey	Individual SOE respondents per country	Number of SOEs per country
Argentina	x	x	11	8
Brazil	x	x	6	6
Canada	x	x	3	1
Chile	x	x	17	11
Colombia	x	x	7	5
Costa Rica		x	10	4
Czech Republic	x	x	8	5
Denmark	x	x	19	9
Finland	x	x	27	10
France	x	x	2	2
Hungary	x	x	12	12
Greece	x			
Iceland	x	x	3	3
Israel		x	1	1
Italy	x	x	9	9
Japan	x			
Kazakhstan	x	x	10	7
Korea	x	x	17	8
Latvia	x	x	38	20
Lithuania		x	3	3
Mexico	x	x	11	7
The Netherlands	x	x	3	3
New Zealand		x	13	6
Norway	x	x	10	5
Pakistan		x	1	1
Paraguay	x			
Peru	x	x	27	12
Philippines	x	x	14	9
Poland	x	x	10	6
Russia		x	5	5
Slovak Republic		x	9	7
Slovenia	x	x	2	2
Spain		x	1	1
Sweden	x	x	9	7
Switzerland	x	x	6	5
Turkey	x	x	18	10
United Kingdom		x	5	3
TOTALS	**28**	**34**	**347**	**213**

Table A A.2. State-owned enterprise respondent sector

Sector	Percentage representation of entire sample
Transportation and Logistics	24.6
Energy (i.e. electricity generation and supply)	19.1
Banking and related financial services	16.5
Oil and Gas	5.5
Information and Communication Technology (ICT)	5.2
Mining	3.5
Agriculture and Fishing	3.2
Postal	3.2
Hospitality and Leisure	2.6
Construction and Engineering	2.3
Health Care	2.3
Real Estate	2.3
Retail and Wholesale	1.7
Manufacturing	1.2
Pensions and Insurance	1.2
Other	5.8

Table A A.3. State-owned enterprise respondent position

Positions of respondents grouped into three main categories reported on

	Percentage representation of entire sample
Heads of the corporate audit, compliance or legal functions	42
Executive management	29
Other	28
Board members	21

Note: Board members included chairs and other board members; executive management included Chief executive officers/presidents/managing directors, chief financial officer or similar or other "c-suite" executives; the group of heads of the corporate audit, compliance or legal functions also included chief risk and chief sustainability officers.

Annex B. OECD 2017 Survey of Anti-Corruption and Integrity in State-Owned Enterprises

Respondent and company information:

*Current position:
Please select the response(s) or responses that best describe your current position, otherwise please select 'other' and state your title. (Note: your responses will remain anonymous to your position and to your company. They will be aggregated with responses of other SOEs in your country).

Chairperson of the Board
Other Board Member
CEO/President/Managing Director
Chief Financial Officer/Treasurer/Comptroller
Chief Audit Executive
Chief Compliance Officer
Chief Risk Officer
Chief Sustainability Officer
Other C-level Executive
Corporate Secretary
Legal Counsel/General Counsel
Other management (Heads of department, administrative manager, quality manager, not specified as C suite)
Other (internal auditor, budget, etc.)

*Are you considered by law as a public official?
Yes
No
I don't know
Other (please specify)

*What is the name of your company:
(Note: this will not be used to identify specific practices by company. Your company name will remain anonymous outside the OECD. This information will help to ensure that double-counting does not happen between multiple anonymous responses within a single company).

*In which country is your company based?

*What sector does your company principally operate in?
Aerospace and Defence
Agriculture and Fishing
Automotive
Banking and related financial services
Chemicals
Communication
Construction and Engineering
Education
Energy (i.e. electricity generation and supply)
Forestry and Timber Products

Hospitality and Leisure
Information Technology (IT)
Manufacturing
Mining
Oil and Gas
Pensions and Insurance
Pharmaceuticals and Medical Devices
Professional Services and Consulting
Real Estate
Retail
Science and Technology
Transportation and Logistics
Other [please specify]:

*How would you classify the objectives of your company?
Entirely commercial
Commercial but subject to legislative or regulatory requirements that may significantly impact profitability
Mixed objectives (commercial with public policy)
Other, please specify

*Are the shares of your company traded in public stock markets?
Yes
No
I don't know
Other

Please specify whether your company is:
Incorporated according to general company law
Incorporated according to legislation guiding state-owned companies in your country
Following legislation specific to your company
I don't know
Other (please specify)

Standards and frameworks for anti-corruption and integrity
The role of the State as owner
*What is the % of government ownership of your company?
< 10
10-19
20-29
30-39
40-49
50-59
60-69
70-79
80-89
90-100

*Can the state intervene in, or veto, company management decisions?
Yes, please specify through which mechanisms
No
I don't know

*How does the state nominate your company's board members (e.g. direct ministerial decision; external HR support, etc.)?

Has your company's state ownership unit/department/agency clearly communicated its expectations for integrity and anti-corruption in your company in the last 12 months?
Yes, please specify through which mechanisms (e.g. written in laws or codes, transmitted through letters/notices, raised in meetings).
No
I don't know

What, if anything, does your company's state ownership unit/department/agency do that is useful in supporting integrity and anti-corruption mechanisms in your company (e.g. holding meetings on the subject, providing guidance, sharing good practices of other companies, supporting identification of corruption risks, etc.)?
Nominations and appointment processes
What is the composition of your company's board or governing body (hereafter referred to only as 'the Board')?

State employees	Number of persons (open text, number)
Other representatives of state	
Employee representatives	
Independents	
Serving politicians	
Other	
My company does not have a board or governing body	

*Does your company have requirements regarding independence of board members (e.g. minimum number of members or minimum ratio of the board; limit on the number of years serving)?
Yes, please specify
No
I don't know

*Please provide any character-based board qualification requirements, or incompatibilities, relating explicitly to integrity or ethics? If this question is left blank, it will be assumed there are no character-based board qualifications relating explicitly to integrity or ethics (open text)

Are the roles of board chair and CEO separate?
Yes
No
I don't know
Other

*Does the board have powers to appoint or remove the CEO?
Yes, please specify whether alone, jointly with the state or subject to state approval?
No
I don't know
Other
Your company's frameworks and standards for integrity
How clearly do relevant national laws, regulations, bylaws or governance codes establish expectations and requirements for your company's actions and responsibilities in areas of integrity and anti-corruption (including for internal control, risk management, compliance etc.)?
Very clearly
Clearly
Somewhat clearly
Not at all clearly
I don't know

Does your company have the following codes or programmes in place that support integrity and anti-corruption? If the question is left blank, it will be assumed that your company does not have any such codes or programmes.
A code of ethics
A code of conduct
A code of compliance
A specific anti-corruption or integrity programme or strategy
Other (please describe)

Please briefly provide further information about such codes or programmes, including whether they were required or established voluntarily, the standards on which they are based (e.g. IIA, COSO, OECD, IFAC, UNCAC, etc.), the goals of the codes/rules, and mechanisms for their implementation and monitoring.

Does your company have particular rules in the following areas?
Conflict of interest
Lobbying
Political party financing or engagement
Charitable contributions and sponsorships
Asset/income disclosure
Public procurement (as bidder)
Public procurement (as procurer of goods and services)
None of the above/not applicable

(Conditional question: IF public procurement as procurer selected) When your company acts as a public procurer (to procure goods and services), is it subject to ordinary government procurement rules?
Yes
No
I don't know
NA
Other (please specify)

(Conditional question: IF public procurement selected as bidder) When your company participates in public procurement bids (i.e. to act as the supplier of goods and services to other parts of the public sector), is it subject to competitive bidding on an equal footing with other firms?
Yes
No
I don't know
NA
Other (please specify)
Company arrangements and approaches to manage integrity and anti-corruption
Operational arrangements and approaches
Do you have any of the following, or similar, specialised board committees related to integrity and anti-corruption matters of your company?
Audit
Compliance
Ethics
Risk management
Procurement
Remuneration
Other similar, please specify
No specialised committees

If your company has the following units or functions, please indicate which of those have significant responsibility for promoting and overseeing integrity or integrity policies (relating to risk, controls, compliance, ethics or anti-corruption mechanisms)? [If the significant responsibility is evenly shared between more than one unit/function, you may select more than one. This question does not refer to the responsibilities of the board in this respect.]

Independent integrity department within your company (e.g. Compliance Unit, Risk Unit, Sustainability Unit)
In-House Legal Department
Internal Audit Department
Internal Controls Department
Internal Human Resources Department
Separate Legal Entity or Special Purpose Vehicle
External Professional Service Provider or Consultant
Other [please specify]:

To whom do those units/functions with significant responsibility for integrity report to? (please check all that apply)
Chairperson of the Board
CEO/President/Managing Director
Board Member
Non-Executive Director
Chief Financial Officer/Treasurer/Comptroller
Chief Audit Executive
Chief Compliance Officer
Chief Risk Officer
Chief Sustainability Officer
Other C-level Executive
Corporate Secretary
Legal Counsel/General Counsel
Other

Please select the activities that are undertaken by these units/functions with significant responsibility for integrity in your company? (please check all that apply)
Developing and maintaining internal guidelines or codes
Overseeing implementation of those internal guidelines or codes
Reviewing/evaluating internal controls and risk-management mechanisms
In-person training
Developing online training
Testing and evaluation
Maintaining and responding to a reporting hotline
Random screening
Ad hoc integrity advice
Internal investigations
Internal audits
Due diligence on third parties
Risk assessments
Reviewing Whistleblower or compliant-mechanism reports
Reporting
Communication with employees/board and senior management/investors/shareholders
Internal remedial/disciplinary action for violation of integrity policies
I don't know
Other [please specify]:

Does your company provide training specifically in integrity or anti-corruption? If such training is not provided to all employees, management and board members, please select "other" and specify who receives it.
Yes, all employees, management and board members receive anti-corruption and integrity training
No, no one receives anti-corruption and integrity training
I don't know if anyone receives anti-corruption and integrity training
Other
Strategic arrangements and approaches
If your company has developed explicit integrity and/or anti-corruption strategies, objectives or indicators, please provide a link or brief details about what those goals, strategies or indicators entail.

*Please estimate the percentage of operational budget that is currently allocated to preventing, detecting and addressing corruption and irregular practices in your company? (Please do not include calculations of cost estimates relating to compliance with enforcement actions or sanctions that have been paid. Please provide number in % form.)

*How would you characterise the allocation of operational budget to preventing, detecting and addressing integrity and anti-corruption?
As an asset/investment
As a cost/expense
I have no view
Other

What were the main motivations behind the current/existing approaches to integrity and anti-corruption in your company? (please select only the factors that had a significant influence on current approaches) (please check all that apply)
Self-driven, voluntary adoption of integrity and anti-corruption measures
Compliance with requirements imposed or requested / regulatory requirements
Change in corporate management
Following a public/media campaign
Following a union movement
Following a corruption scandal
Risk of personal liability of CEO or senior management
Risk of reputational damage
Risk of legal or enforcement action, or divestment by investors
Risk of legal or enforcement action by shareholders
Risk of debarment or exclusion to processes
Risk of potential corrupt acts or irregular practices
Risk of loss of earnings

Internal control, risk management and compliance
Please select the following integrity-related findings/recommendations/assessments that are brought to the attention of your company's leadership (board and senior management)? If the item does not exist in your company, please select "does not exist".
Findings of risk assessments that point to integrity or corruption risks
Internal audit findings/recommendations
External audit findings/recommendations
Recommendations from integrity functions
Reports or claims of irregular practices or corruption made through reporting channels
Evaluations of the board
Evaluations of senior management (c-suite)
Evaluations of internal controls (that may be separate from internal audits)
Other inputs, please specify

*Under which category of risks does your company categorise integrity or anti-corruption risks, if at all?
Strategic risk factors
Operational risk factors
Financial risk factors
Compliance risk factors
Separately (please specify)
Such risks are not explicitly treated
Other, please specify:

How often does your company generally conduct risk assessments aimed specifically at identifying, analysing and prioritising corruption risks?
Never
Annually
Every two to three years
Every 4-5 years

More than 5 years
I don't know

*Which additional risk management mechanisms or tools/instruments does your company use, if any, for protecting your company's integrity when operating with third parties, or in high-risk sectors (i.e. mining or extractive, construction) or activities (i.e. public procurement)? (e.g. ex ante risk assessment of proposals/third parties, collective action agreements, anti-corruption agreements or integrity pacts, certifying business coalitions, and collective engagement with governments or others (including civil society)).
Accountability
Liability regime
What is the liability regime of your company for corruption or irregular practices?
Your company as an entity is not liable at all
Your company as an entity is liable only when senior management (in the "directing mind" and will of the company) committed the crime (sometimes known as the identification doctrine or theory)
Your company as an entity is liable for wrongdoing by all officers, directors/board members, employees or agents acting within their employment and for the benefit of the company (sometimes known as vicarious or strict liability)
Your company as an entity is liable for failure to prevent wrongdoing, but allows for a defence of the company to demonstrate that it had adequate compliance or related procedures in place to prevent misconduct (sometimes known as partial or adjusted strict liability)
Other [please specify]:

Please list any company positions (e.g. board members, CFO, CEO) that are exempt from the application of your company's liability regime?
Internal and external audit
*Please best describe your company's internal audit unit/function:
Required, in line with government departments/agencies
Required, in line with listed companies
Required, in line with other privately incorporated companies
Voluntarily established
Not applicable/do not have internal audit
Other

(Ask only if NOT said "yes" to IA as IF) To whom does the internal audit function/unit report? (please select all that apply)
Board
Audit committee (if existing)
Senior management
Other [please specify]:

Which types of internal audits are undertaken in your company? Select all that apply.
Performance audits (efficiency, effectiveness and economy of operations)
Compliance audits (compliance with legal norms and standards)
Financial audits (audit of financial reports and reporting processes)
Other audits (please specify)

Transparency
Does your company publicly disclose/report the following material financial and non-financial information on the enterprise? (if none of the above, please specify what other material financial or non-financial information is disclosed). (please select all that apply)

A clear statement to the public of enterprise objectives and their fulfilment
Enterprise financial and operating results
The governance, ownership and voting structure of the enterprise
The remuneration of board members and key executives;
Board member qualifications and selection process
Any board evaluations

Any material foreseeable risk factors and measures taken to manage such risks;
Any financial assistance, including guarantees, received from the state and commitments made on behalf of your company
Any material transactions with the state and other related entities;
Other, please specify

Through which sources/documentation does your company report on its integrity policies or anti-corruption efforts? (please select all that apply)
Annual Report
Compliance Report
CSR/Sustainability Report
Information published on organisation website
Internal documents only
Information is not reported
I don't know
Other [please specify]:
Self-reporting and whistleblowing mechanisms
Which mechanisms are made available to internal and/or external persons to report suspected instances of corruption or irregular practices involving your company? (please select all that apply)
Online (internal site)
Online (external site)
Telephone (internal hotline)
Telephone (external hotline)
Formalised whistleblowing mechanism
In person, ombudsman
In person, other
Other [please specify]:

*Please estimate how many reports/claims have been made through these channels in the last year, and how many pertain to corruption and irregular practices? (please respond in numeric characters)

How are internal and external reports/claims about corruption or irregular practices categorised/classified when coming through your company's reporting mechanism?
Anonymously
Confidentially
Attributed to the individuals who made them when discussed within the organisation
I don't know
Other [please specify]:

To whom are reports and claims channelled to / who receives them? (please select all that apply)
External service provider
Board
Board committee
CEO
Chief Audit Executive
Chief Compliance Officer
Chief Financial Officer
Chief Sustainability Officer
General Counsel
External counsel (i.e. private legal practitioner)
Human Resources Department
Union Representative
Other [please specify]:

Does your company have legal protection from discriminatory or disciplinary action for those who disclose wrongdoing in good faith, to competent authorities, on reasonable grounds?
Yes, required by law
Yes, voluntary
No
I don't know

(If yes) Please describe how this written policy is effectively guaranteed (e.g. retaliation as grounds for discipline up to and including dismissal?)
Specific company integrity and anti-corruption risks
In your opinion, to what degree does each factor pose as an obstacle to effectively promoting integrity and preventing corruption in, or involving, your company? (please respond in view of your specific company's existing/true risks and its operations, not hypothetical. If the below factors are not present or do not exist in your company, please select "not applicable/does not exist". If they exist, but do not pose an obstacle, please select "not at all an obstacle".)
Matrix question:

A lack of a culture of integrity in the political and public sector	Is it an obstacle? Very much an obstacle An obstacle Somewhat of an obstacle Not at all an obstacle NA/Does not exist
A lack of a culture of integrity in your company	
A lack of awareness among employees of the need for, or priority placed on, integrity	
A lack of awareness of legal requirements	
Conflicting corporate objectives	
Inadequate financial or human resources to invest in integrity and prevent corruption	
Inadequate remuneration/compensation	
Ineffective channels for whistleblowing / reporting misconduct	
Ineffective internal audit	
Ineffective external audit	
Ineffective internal control or risk management	
Loyalty to company	
Loyalty to customers or third parties	
Perceived cost of corruption is low and/or return is high	
Perceived likelihood of getting caught is low	
Pressure to perform or meet targets	
Pressure to rule-break	
Overly complex or burdensome legal requirements	
Opportunistic behaviour of individuals	
Relations between your company, or the board, and political officials	
Unclear or ineffective reporting lines between integrity units and Board and others	
Unclear rules or guidance from the government ownership entity	
Unsupportive leadership from the Board or management	
Fear of "doing the right thing"	
Other [please specify]:	

In your personal assessment, please rate the below integrity risks for their likelihood of materialising/occurring and the impact they would have on your company? The responses will be aggregated with other participating companies, not linked to any one company. (Likelihood is the possibility/probability that a risk event may occur in, or involving, your company. Impact is the affect that the risk event would have on achievement of your company's desired results or objectives. For instance, high impact would have a severe impact on achieving desired results, such that one or more of its critical outcome objectives will not be achieved. Low impact would have little or no impact on achieving outcome objectives.)
Matrix question:

Anti-competitive, anti-trust activities or collusive activities	Likelihood: High Medium Low Impact: High Medium Low
Abusive or intimidating behaviour towards employees	
(Receiving) bribes	
(Offering) bribes	
Favouritism (nepotism, cronyism and patronage)	
Fraud	
Illegal information brokering	
Falsification and/or misrepresentation of company documents, or false accounting	
Influence peddling	
Interference in appointments of board members or CEO	
Interference in decision-making	
(Receiving) kickbacks and/or inappropriate gifts	
(Offering) kickbacks and/or inappropriate gifts	
Lying to employees, customers, vendors or the public	
Non-declaration of conflict of interest	
Money laundering	
Procurement/contract violations (delivering sub-par goods/services, violating contract terms with suppliers)	
Making political party donations	
Retaliation against someone who has reported misconduct	
Stealing or theft of goods from your company	
Trading in influence	
Violations of data protection and privacy	
Violations of Intellectual Property Rights	
Violations of regulations (health and safety, environmental)	
Other, please specify	

*In your assessment, did any of the above risks materialise into activities/actions in the last three years in (or involving) your company?
Yes
No
I don't know

(Conditional Question: IF "yes" selected to above question) Which actors(s) was(were) involved in the above activities/actions that materialised? Please check all that apply, recalling that the survey results will not be linked to your specific company.
Public official
Business partner
Civil society representative
Shareholder
Board
Senior management (c-suite)
Mid-level management
Employee

(Conditional * Question: IF "yes" selected to above question) **When the above risks materialised into activities/actions, did you report them?
Yes
No
I don't know
Other (please specify)

(Conditional Question: IF "no" selected to above question) why not?

(Conditional Question: IF "yes" selected to above question) Did you face retaliation for reporting that the above risks materialised into activities/actions?
Yes, please elaborate
No
I don't know

What, if any, are the particular risks for your company in engaging in public procurement? If not applicable, please leave blank.

*Please estimate the share of annual corporate profits that is lost due to irregular practices and corruption (This figure may include cost estimates relating to compliance with enforcement actions or sanctions that have been paid) (please provide number as a % of total profits)

*Has your company's leadership (board or senior management) taken the following actions in the last three years?
Matrix question:

Severed a relationship with at least one business partner (e.g. supplier, service provider) because of the risk of exposure to or engaging in corruption?	Yes No I don't know Other (please specify)
Ceased business operations in a particular jurisdiction because of the integrity or corruption risks involved?	
Substantially revised at least one business project because of the corruption and integrity risk(s) involved?	
Taken internal remedial/disciplinary action following violation of your organisation's integrity or anti-corruption policies?	

ORGANISATION FOR ECONOMIC CO-OPERATION AND DEVELOPMENT

The OECD is a unique forum where governments work together to address the economic, social and environmental challenges of globalisation. The OECD is also at the forefront of efforts to understand and to help governments respond to new developments and concerns, such as corporate governance, the information economy and the challenges of an ageing population. The Organisation provides a setting where governments can compare policy experiences, seek answers to common problems, identify good practice and work to co-ordinate domestic and international policies.

The OECD member countries are: Australia, Austria, Belgium, Canada, Chile, the Czech Republic, Denmark, Estonia, Finland, France, Germany, Greece, Hungary, Iceland, Ireland, Israel, Italy, Japan, Korea, Latvia, Lithuania, Luxembourg, Mexico, the Netherlands, New Zealand, Norway, Poland, Portugal, the Slovak Republic, Slovenia, Spain, Sweden, Switzerland, Turkey, the United Kingdom and the United States. The European Union takes part in the work of the OECD.

OECD Publishing disseminates widely the results of the Organisation's statistics gathering and research on economic, social and environmental issues, as well as the conventions, guidelines and standards agreed by its members.

OECD PUBLISHING, 2, rue André-Pascal, 75775 PARIS CEDEX 16
(21 2018 02 1 P) ISBN 978-92-64-30304-1 – 2018

www.ingramcontent.com/pod-product-compliance
Lightning Source LLC
Chambersburg PA
CBHW061218240926
51846CB00006B/1264
* 9 7 8 9 2 6 4 3 0 3 0 4 1 *